Prayers for Today's Journey
By: Minister Debra Coleman-LeBum

To my sister + brother Edith + Charles Still,

Thank you so much for your love + support. You have been such an inspiration to me. Words can not express my love + gratitude to you both. Know that I love you both very much.

Love,
Minister Debra Coleman-LeBum
0/0

All rights reserved. Excerpt for brief quotations used in reviews, articles, or other media, no parts of this book may be reproduced or transmitted in any form without permission from the publisher or author.

Scriptures quotations are taken from:

The Holy Bible, New International Version (NIV) Copyright @ 1973, 1978, 1984 by International Bible Society. Used by permission of Zondervan Publishing House. All rights reserved.

The Holy Bible, The Message Bible (MSG) This edition by contractual arrangements with NavPress, a division of The Navigators. U.S.A. Originally published by NavPress in English as THE MESSAGE: The Bible in Contemporary Language copyright 2002-2003 by Eugene Peterson. All rights reserved.

The New American Standard Bible (NASB) @ 1960, 1962, 1968, 1971, 1972, 1973, 1975, 1977, 1995 by Lockman Foundation. Used by permission.

Published by: Lulu Publishing Company
Cover Design by Demond Woodard
    Printed in the United States of America

ISBN 978-0557-24723-3

Content

Introduction

Dedication

Forward by First Lady Gayle Woodard – CRM City Fellowship Church

   Trusting in God

   Bear our Burdens

   Cast your cares

   Taking Refuge

   Rejoice in the Lord

   Foot will not stumble

   Power that work within

   My cup of Blessing

   Anxious about anything

   Have mercy Lord

   Loving your enemies

   Righteous Person

Introduction

  To God be the Glory for all that he has done, and all that he is about to do in the life of his people. God gave me this title in 2003. It was a time that my family was going through in the loss of my grandmother and my mother. Who passed away two months apart. It was a very difficult time for all of my family members. Nevertheless, God still worked it out for all of us. We still have our moments when we remember something they said or done, but God is healing each of us. So to my family I would like to say be encouraged and continue to look to the hills from whence cometh your help, your help cometh from the Lord.

  My grandmother (Ocie Brite) who had raised me until I was 12 years old had passed away. My grandmother was the backbone of my family. She was a very strong woman who loved the Lord with all her heart. She taught me to love everyone that I met, no matter what color, creed, or nationality. We are all God's children. She was well known for her homemade cakes, and for keeping her children and grandchildren together. My grandmother who was one of my inspirations for writing this book and the prayers on the emails to all.

  The other person who inspired me and who I loved with all my heart and soul was my mother (Savanna Mae Brite Powell bka Dorsell). My mother was such an inspiration to me in many ways. My mother taught me what it meant in the Bible when Jesus said, when I was hungry did you feed me, when I needed shelter did you give me shelter, when I need clothing, did you clothe me. Because you see my mother always, welcomed anyone into our home no matter what the circumstances was. I remember a time in my life, when we had no food, all we had were each other and love. She would go to the food pantry and get us food.

No matter how much we had in our home, we always shared with someone. She taught me how to lean and depend on Jesus for everything I needed in life. She had the kind of faith that would move mountains. She loved her family and her children, and grandchildren so much. Both of these women will be missed. They are gone, but not forgotten.

My husband has played a big role in helping me to birth out this book as well. My husband (Alfred W. LeBum Sr.) has inspired me to hold on and to go on in the Lord. It was a time in our marriage when all hell was breaking out. We had separated and God begin to deal with both of us on a spiritual level. My husband has the kind of faith that would move any mountain. I am talking about a man who does not allow the cares of this world to worry him. A man who loves the Lord with all his heart and soul. A man who does not mind serving God and others. A man after God's own heart. He has prayed me through some very difficult times in my life. Through sickness, through heartache and pain he comforted me with the words of wisdom that God has given him. When I look back over his life and see where he use to be and where he is now, it truly blesses me to know that God did all that to him. I thank God for my husband and the strength that God has given him. When you have been through so much pain and sorrow and you do not know where to turn to, I tell you there is power in the name of Jesus. God has been my strength and my inspiration along the way. Through all the good times, the bad times, and through the death of my love ones. I also would like to say that my children have been an inspiration to me as well. Reginald, Mary, Marquita, Chanikka, and Alfred Jr. (JR) I love you all very much. Keep God first in your life and you will reach your destiny in life.

In 2003 after the passing of my grandmother and my mother, I begin to pray and ask God how I could help heal my family. He told me to start sending out prayers to all those who I had an email address to each day. To let my family know that once they received the email that they had to share the pray with other family members. It started out being just my family for a while, and then God told me to open it up to family and friends. Now I send these prayers to every walk of the world. People that I don't even know have emailed me and told me how the prayers for that day has been a blessing to them, or how it has encouraged them to hold on a little while longer. I give all the glory and honor to God for using me to touch lives all across the world. After praying and seeking God for almost two and half years, here I am today still giving my Father the glory for all that he has brought my family through. Prayer does change things. Prayer is the key that unlock the supernatural blessings that are from God. I thank God for all that he has done in my life. I know that if it had not been for God on my side I would not be where I am today.

Many times, I will be at my computer praying for encouraging words to send and God will speak to me and begin to reveal something that is going on in someone life, and I begin to minister to that person through the prayers. Sometimes it is persons that I do not know or someone that received the email from someone else. I have the satisfactions of knowing that God's word is being delivered via email to all walks of the world.

To you who have purchased this book, I hope and pray that God will speak to you and your situations through these prayers. I hope these prayers will encourage your heart and draw you closer to God, our Father. That you will have a closer relationship with him like never before. It is my prayer and my wish that this book will enlighten and strengthen someone in their walk with God.

May God bless you and keep you strong spiritually, mentally, emotionally, and physically. To God be the glory.

Minister Debra Coleman- LeBum

Dedication of this book

"I can do all things through Christ who strengthen me."
(Philippians 4:13)

    First, I would like to give honor and praise to my Father, the Almighty God, who has blessed me with the wisdom, knowledge and understanding of his word to reach out to the lost through prayer.

    I dedicated this book to the memory of my grandmother (Ocie Mae Brite) and my mother (Savanna Mae Brite).

    To my husband (Alfred LeBum Sr.) thank you for your love, your support, your understanding and your patience. Thanks for believing in me, to do what I need to do for God.

    To my children, and grandchildren, I love you dearly. Thanks for standing by my side. I love you all.

    To my family, my brothers, my sister, my aunts, my uncles, my cousins, godchildren, god-family, and my extended family members. Thank you for being my inspiration, and for your love.

    To my Pastor Leroy J. Woodard Jr. and First Lady Gayle Woodard, thank you so much for entrusting me with the prayer ministry at the church and for helping me to get to the next level in God. Thank you for your love, your support, your friendship. God bless you.

To Demond Woodard who designed the cover to this project. Thank you for taking my vision and putting it on paper. God bless you.

My spiritual mothers & fathers in this ministry, I love you all. Thanks for covering me in prayer daily.

To CRM City Fellowship Church my church family. Words cannot express my love for each of you. I love you. Thank you for giving me the awesome task of interceding for you and your family.

To all those who have received an email prayer on a weekly basis I want to thank you for allowing the Holy Spirit to speak through me to you. God bless each of you.

Foreword by

First Lady Gayle Woodard - CRM City Fellowship Church

To my Sister Debra LeBum, my spiritual daughter and an awesome prayer warrior. I thank God for you and the many prayers that you have prayed and interceded for others. You are incredible women of God and I believe that this book will be a tremendous blessing to the Body of Christ and people all over the world. You are a woman of faith, hope, and prayer. A woman that walks along side her husband, as a Deacon's wife. The many prayer that you have prayed for others, it is time to be blessed. I pray God's blessings over your life. The CRM Church family especially the Woodland Campus are so encouraged by your intercessory prayer, the prayer grams, fasting, and praying time, truly has made a difference to the body of Christ. You have impacted the lives of others through your prayer ministry. I thank God for your wonderful love and support and prayers for Pastor and I and our sons. I am very proud of you and what God is doing in your life.

God bless you

Lady Gayle Woodard

"Trust in him at all times, O people; pour out your hearts to him, for God is our refuge. Selah" (Psalm 62:8) NIV

My God,

     God you are awesome. Lord, you are my all and all I worship and adore you. I love you and I glorify your holy name. Thank you Father for your wonder working power. Thank you for your edge of protection. I just want to tell you Lord, that I love you more than anything in this world. Lord, my trust is in you for every situation that I face each day of my life. You told me to put my trust in you and not in man. When I look back over the things that I went through thus far, I realize it was because I had put my trust in man and not in you. It is so hard to trust when you have been hurt. People lie on you. They even say things about you to others that you have not even done or said, so that they may look good I guess. Then because of what they have said people will not like you or they to will talk about you to someone else. Lord, help me to trust again. Help me to see the good in people through your eyesight and not mine. Lord, you alone are my rock and my salvation. You alone are my fortress, and I will not be shaken by my circumstances. My soul finds rest in the Lord, because my salvation comes from the Lord. My salvation and my honor depend on God, it is not my circumstances, nor my situation, but it is God that I depend on. Thank you Jesus. Lord, help me not to trust in exhortation or take pride in stolen goods, though my riches increase, I will not set my heart on those things. One thing that God has spoken, two things have I heard; that God is strong, and God is a loving God. Surely, He will reward each person according to what he has done. Thank you Jesus. Forgive me Lord, for not allowing your word to get deep into my spirit. Forgive those who I have been holding something against, and likewise forgive me. Lead me not into temptation, but deliver me from the evil one. You are so worthy Lord. You are great. Thank you for your loving kindness, and your patience to endure until the end. In Jesus name, I pray. Amen

Praise be to the Lord, to God our Savior, who daily bears our burdens. Selah Our God is a God who saves; from the Sovereign Lord comes escape from death." (Psalm 68:19-20) NIV

My God,

You are worthy of the praise and the glory. God, you are awesome. Lord, I will forever lift my eyes to thee in total gratitude. Your word is so true. For you said in your word that you never seen the righteous forsaken nor his seed begging for bread. Your word is a light unto my pathway. Because I am a seed and a child of the most high king, my children are my seeds, and they shall not be forsaken nor shall they beg for bread. God shall cover them and keep them out of all hurt, harm and danger. He shall protect them and guide them into all righteousness. Though they slay me, yet will I trust in him. Though my enemies try to do me wrong, I can declare and decree that no weapon formed against my household shall prosper. I decree and declare that my children are blessed and their children are blessed in the mighty name of Jesus. Lord, I thank you for your wonder working power to defeat the enemy at his own game. Lord, you are good, and you are great, there is nothing hidden under the sun that you cannot and will not reveal unto your people. There is no prison cell, nor any walls that can keep your children from getting what is rightful there's through your word. Thank you Jesus, for your word and your promises for my family and me. Lord, forgive me for any sins that I may have committed and forgive those who are holding something against me. Lead me not into temptation but deliver me from the evil one. For you alone are worthy and powerful. I give you all the praise and the glory in Jesus name I pray. Amen

"Cast your cares on the Lord and he will sustain you; he will never let the righteous fall. But you, O God, will bring down the wicked into the pit of corruption; bloodthirsty and deceitful men will not live out half their days. But as for me, I trust in you." (Psalm 55:22-23) NIV

My God,

The King of kings, and the lords of Lords, how great you are. You are my Jehovah Jireh, my provider. You are the author and finisher of my faith. You made me out of your image, and I am thankful. Lord, there are many things I take for granted. May I have not ignore them today. Just for today, help me God, to remember that my life is a gift, that my health is a blessing, that this new day is filled with awesome potential, that I have the capacity to bring something new, unique and good into this world. Just for today, help me, God, to remember to be kind and patient to the people who love me, and to those who work with me too. Teach me to see all the beauty that I so often ignore, and to listen to the silent longing of my own soul. Thank you God, for the body you have given me. Most of the time I take my health for granted. I forget how fortunate I am to live without pain or disability, how blessed I am to be able to see and hear and walk and eat. I forget that this body of mine, with all its imperfections is a gift from you. When I am critical of my appearance, remind me, God, that I am created in your holy image. If I become jealous of someone else's appearance, teach me to treasure my unique form. Help me, God, to care for my body. Teach me to refrain from any action that will bring harm to me. If I prey to a self-destruction habit, fill me with the strength to conquer my cravings. Lead me to use my body wisely, God. Guide my every limb, God, to perform acts of compassion and kindness. Forgive me if I am complaining, or not being thankful enough. Forgive those who I may have offended. Lead me not into temptation, but deliver me from the evil one. You are great Lord. You are worthy of all praise and glory in the name of Jesus I pray. Amen.

"It is better to take refuge in the Lord, than to trust in man. It is better you take refuge in the Lord, than to trust in princes." (Psalm 118:8-9) NIV

My Father,

O Lord, my God how excellent is your name in all the earth. You have set your glory above the heavens. My soul blesses you and I remember all your benefits. You are the one who forgives all my sins, heal me from diseases, redeem my life from destruction, and crown me with tender mercy. You fill my life with good things and renew my youth like the eagles! I honor you as my Lord and Savior. Lord, I do not want to be a burden. I certainly do not want pity. But I no longer can do it all alone. Help me, God. Teach me not to be afraid to rely upon others. Show me how to accept kindness, how to ask for help. Teach me, God, that my children still love me even though they are grown. I still have so much to offer, Lord. Help me find the ways to transmit my wisdom, to share my love, to realize my talents, to offer my reassurance and support to others. Most of all, I place all my trust in You, Lord; I place my body and soul in your hands, and pray that you will be with me each step of the way. Guide my every limb, Lord, to perform acts of compassion and kindness. Thank You for loving me, and caring for me even when I have ignore you and gone my own way. Forgive me for not always listening to what you have said to me. Lead me not into temptation, but deliver me from the evil one. In Jesus name, I pray. Amen

"The Lord has done this, and it is marvelous in our eyes. This is the day the Lord has made; let us rejoice and be glad in it." (Psalm 118: 23-24) NIV

Heavenly Father,

You are a great and merciful Father. I bless your name today. By your awesome power, you made the earth and have established this world by your infinite wisdom. You are the Lord who stretched out the heavens at your discretion. Lord, you are great. Thank You for blessing me with abundance, peace, and security. Father, it is your will that I walk by faith and not by sight. I know that faith is the substance of things hoped for, the evidence of things not seen. Father, I ask you to please be attentive to my prayer. Forgive me for not believing that all things are possible through Jesus Christ who strengthens me.
Forgive me for walking in doubt, unbelief, arrogance, and pride. Forgive me for not keeping my spirit man strong and vibrant in your word. Lord, remind me of those I need to forgive, and help me to be quick to forgive. Lead us not into temptation; but deliver us from the evil one. Lord, you are the blessed and only Sovereign One. You are the King of kings and Lord of lords, who rides on the heaven of heavens, which are of old! O God, You are more awesome than your holy places. You are the God of Israel who gives strength and power to His people. Blessed are you, forever. In Jesus' name, Amen.

"Then you will go on your way in safety, and your foot will not stumble; when you lie down, you will not be afraid; when you lie down, your sleep will be sweet." (Proverbs 3: 23-24)NIV

Father, in the Name of Jesus, I thank you that you watch over Your Word to perform it.

Father, I praise you that I may dwell in the secret place of the Most High and that I shall remain stable and fixed under the shadow of the Almighty. - Whose power no foe can withstand. I will say of You, Lord, "The Lord is my refuge and my fortress, my God; on Him I lean and rely, and in Him I confidently trust!" For then you will deliver me from the snare of the fowler and from the deadly pestilence. Then you will cover me with your feathers, and under your wings, shall I trust and find refuge. Your truth and your faithfulness are a shield and a buckler. Father, you are my confidence, firm and strong. You keep my foot from stumbling, being caught in a trap, or hidden danger. Father, you give me safety and ease me. I know you will keep me in perfect peace because my mind is stayed on you and I trust in you. I thank You, Lord, that I may lie down and you will give me peaceful sleep, for you sustain me and make me dwell in safety. I shall not be afraid of the terror of the night, nor of the arrow (the evil plots and slanders of the wicked) that flies by day, nor of the pestilence that stalks in darkness, nor of the destruction and sudden death that surprise and lay waste at noonday. A thousand may fall at my side, and ten thousand at my right hand, but it shall not come near me. Only a spectator shall I be - inaccessible in the secret place of the Most High - as I witness the reward of the wicked. Because I have made You, Lord, my refuge, and the Most High my dwelling place, there shall no evil befall me, nor any plague or calamity come near my tent. For you will give your angels special charge over me, to accompany, defend, and preserve me in all my ways of obedience and service. They are encamped around about me. Your angels shall bear me up on their hands, lest I dash my foot against a stone. I shall tread upon the lion and adder; the young lion and the dragon shall I trample underfoot. Because I have set my love upon you, therefore will you deliver me. You will set me on high, because I know and understand your name. I have a personal knowledge of your mercy, love and kindness. I trust and rely on you, knowing you will never forsake me, no, never. I shall call upon you, and you will answer me. You will be with me in trouble. You will deliver me and honor me. With long life, will you satisfy me and show me your salvation! Thank you Lord for your edge of protection over my family. In the mighty name of Jesus, I pray. Amen

"Now to him who is able to do immeasurably more than all we ask or imagine, according to his power that is at work within us, to him be glory in the church and in Christ Jesus throughout all generations, for ever and ever! Amen" (Ephesians 3:20-21) NIV

My Father and God of our Lord Jesus Christ,

Father of glory, I ask that you give to me the spirit of wisdom and revelation in the knowledge of You; the eyes of my understanding being enlightened, that I may know what is the hope of Your calling, and what are the riches of the glory of Your inheritance in the saints. For this cause I bow my knees to You, Lord Jesus, of whom the whole family in heaven and earth are named. That you would grant me according to Your riches in glory. To be strengthened with might in the inner man; that Christ may live in my heart by faith. That I being rooted and grounded in love, may be able to comprehend with all the saints, what is the breadth and length and depth and height of your word. To know the love of Christ that passes all knowledge, that I might be filled with all the fullness of God. Now unto Him that is able to do exceedingly abundantly above all that we ask or think, according to the power that worketh in me, unto Him be glory in the church by Christ Jesus throughout all ages, world without end. Amen

"I said to the Lord, "You are my Master!" All the good things I have are from you"... Lord, you alone are my inheritance, my cup of blessing. You guard all that is mine. The land you have given me is a pleasant land. What a wonderful inheritance!" (Psalm 16:2, 5-6) NIV

God, you are awesome, wonderful, and adored by all. You are the beginning and the end. You are my Jehovah Riveh, my El Shadai, my all and all. I bow down and worship you. I give you all the praise and the glory. Lord, we've all heard of families who are divided forever because they disagreed over an inheritance. Brothers and sisters who once loved each other spend the rest of their lives greedily fighting to protect what they have inherited from their parents, while others go to their graves hating and resenting their siblings who got a bigger share than they did. How refreshing to hear David say to the Lord, "The land you have given me is a pleasant land. What a wonderful inheritance!" Am I satisfied with what the Lord has given me, no matter how great or small? Can I say, and really mean it, "I have you, Lord, and that's enough"? When I list in my mind all that God has given me. I truly am blessed. Because he has given me life. He has given me his word to live by daily. He has given me health. He has given me a loving spouse. He has given me beautiful children, and grandchildren. He has given me a home. He has given me a car to drive. He has given me a family who pray together. He has given me a job. He has given me a pastor who lives by the word he teaches. Who is also a friend, and a brother. He has given me all that I need to survive in this life. These are some of my inheritance that I am thankful for. I can rejoice over my inheritance, over all the good things God has given me. Lord, you alone are my inheritance. All the good things I have are from you. I give you the praise and the glory and I thank you for given me exceedingly more than I could ever ask for or even think of, I give you the glory. In the mighty name of Jesus, I pray. Amen

"Do not be anxious about anything, but in everything, by prayer and petition with thanksgiving, present your requests to God. And the peace of God, which transcends all understanding, will guard your hearts and your minds in Christ Jesus." (Philippians 4:6-7) NIV

My God,

Lord, you are awesome, and wonderful. You are great, and mighty. You are marvelous, and powerful. You reign on the just and the unjust. You are omnipresent. You are my all and all. I worship and adore you. Thank You Lord, for all that you do and all that you are about to do not just in my life but in my families life as well. Thank You for your love and your protection. Lord, please put your peace in my heart. I'm worried and anxious. My mind races and obsesses. I can't help thinking about my problems. And the more I think about them, the more depressed I become. I feel like I'm sinking down in quicksand and can't get out. Calm me, Lord. Slow me down, put your peace in my heart. No matter what problem I have, Lord, you are bigger, you are more powerful than it is. So I bring my problem to you. I know what I want. I know my will. I do not know yours. I do not know how you will use this problem for my salvation. I do not know what good you will workout at this point. But I trust you. I trust your goodness and your wisdom. So I place myself in your hands. Please fill my heart with peace. Touch every situation in my life that has become a problem and has caused me to worry about it. I release it all into your mighty hands Lord. Now, Lord, forgive me for worrying and allowing myself to fall into depression when I know that is an attack from the enemy. Let this mind, Lord be in you be also in Christ Jesus. Lord, I thank you and I praise you for all that I have gone through and all that you are doing to help me release it. In the mighty name of Jesus, I pray. Amen

"I lift my eye to you, O God, enthroned in heaven. We look to the Lord our God for his mercy; just a servant keeps their eyes on their master, as a slave girl watches her mistress for the slightest signal. Have mercy on us, Lord, have mercy, for we have had our fill of contempt." (Psalm 123:1-3) NIV

Oh Lord,

You are great. You are wonderful. You are my all and all and to you I give the glory and the honor forever. One of the most difficult things to do in life is waiting... My desire is to have the finished product or get to my intended goal immediately. But the psalmist in this prayer knew that waiting on the Lord was best, so he was going to wait as long as it took to see God's mercy revealed in his life. God grants us mercy, not because we deserve it but because he loves me, and he will grant it in his own timing. Like servants who keep their eyes on their master or a slave girl who watches her mistress for the slightest signal, I should be attentive to God's leading and patiently wait on God for his help. Lord, I lift my eyes to you and look to you for mercy. I wait expectantly for you to help me. Lord, I thank you for your kindness and mercy toward me today. I thank you for forgiving me of my sins, and helping me to forgive others as well. Lead me not into temptation, but deliver me from the evil one. I will forever give your name the praise and the glory in Jesus name I pray. Amen.

"But I tell you who hear me: Love your enemies, do good to those who hate you, bless those who curse you, pray for those who mistreat you. If someone strikes you on one cheek, turn to him the other also. If someone takes your cloak, do not stop him from taking your tunic. Give to everyone who asks you, and if anyone takes what belongs to you, do not demand it back. Do to others, as you would have them do to you.
"If you love those who love you, what credit is that to you? Even 'sinners' love those who love them. And if you do good to those who are good to you, what credit is that to you? Even 'sinners' do that. And if you lend to those from whom you expect repayment, what credit is that to you? Even 'sinners' lend to 'sinners,' expecting to be repaid in full. But love your enemies, do good to them, and lend to them without expecting to get anything back. Then your reward will be great, and you will be sons of the Most High, because he is kind to the ungrateful and wicked. Be merciful, just as your Father is merciful." (Luke 6:27-36) NIV

Heavenly Father,

    I ask that you bless my enemy. Bless my enemy with the peace that I seek. Fill my enemy with the love for those around him that I desire. Grant my enemy the patience in facing adversity that I long for. Give my enemy the faith that I desire, bless his/her efforts at glorifying God, that mind are pathetic by comparison. Make my enemies presence a source of joy to all who are near them, and may the sound of their voice heal all who hear it. May my enemy's prayers be such fine incense to you Lord, that mine are contemptible. Grant my enemy each spiritual gift that I desire in my childish greed, give to them twofold. Fill my enemy with wisdom and insight for every situation. Bless my enemy with good health; heal him of every physical, emotional, and spiritual illness. Bless my enemy with joy and happiness. Bless my enemy with the best of friends, fellowship, and family. Give my enemy job fulfillment, job security, and a pleasant working environment. Grant my enemy a life filled with physical comfort, home, wealth, independence; all of the possessions I would ask. Father, for every sin that my enemy has committed, let me be the one punished. Let every blow meant for my enemy, every act of degradation that any desire for him, fall on me. Please let every angry word meant for my enemy, on me. Let every hateful, resentful, loathing, thought directed at my enemy, be mine alone to bear. Lord, I thank you for blessing my enemies, and giving them the desire to walk upright in your word. Let your love Lord fill any empty void in their live right now in the mighty name of Jesus. Let others love on them just as you Lord love each of us. Thank you for your grace and your mercy in Jesus' name, Amen.

"Finally, all of you, live in harmony with one another; be sympathetic, love as brothers, be compassionate and humble. Do not repay evil with evil or insult with insult, but with blessing, because to this you were called so that you may inherit a blessing." (1 Peter 3:8-9) NIV

My God;

   Lord, our refuge and strength, listen to my praise at the beginning of this day, in you, I place my faith and hope, and you know my needs. Remember the poor and unfortunate. Lord, I thank you for the many times you gave me help, always listening when I called. In my darkest moments, when all seemed to be lost, there you were at my side. I may for a time have to suffer the distress of many trials; but this is so that my faith, which is more precious than the passing splendor of fire-tried gold, may by its genuineness lead to praise, glory, and honor when Jesus Christ appears. I praise You, God my Father, for the life you give me today. I praise you for Your Son who fills me with wisdom and knowledge. I praise you, my Father of mercy, for preserving me from temptation each day. I love you and adore you. I worship and bow down before you. I exalt your Holy name. I give you all the praise for every thing that you have done in my life, and for my family in the mighty name of Jesus I Pray. Amen.

"The Bible says that the prayer of the righteous person is powerful and effective. (James 5:17)   The word of God is living and active, sharper than any double-edged sword. (Hebrews 4:12) God watches over his word to see that it is fulfilled. (Jeremiah 1:12) NIV

My Lord;
   You are the Lord of peace. Please give us your peace at all times and in every way. (2 Thessalonians 3:16)
 Help us to cast our cares on you, knowing that you will sustain us. You never let the righteous fall. (Psalms 55:12)
 Please keep us in perfect peace because our mind is fixed steadfastly on you, and we trust in you. (Isaiah 26:3)
 Answer us when we call, righteous God. Give us relief from our distress. Be merciful to us and hear our prayers. (Psalms 4:1) Help us not to be anxious about anything. In everything, by prayer and petition, with thanksgiving, let us present our requests to you. We thank you that your peace, which transcends all understanding, will keep our hearts and minds in Christ Jesus. (Philippians 4:6, 7) Help us to be strong and take heart, because our hope is in you, Lord. (Psalms 31:24) Enable us to cast all our anxiety on you, because you care for us. (1 Peter 5:7) Lord, you are a refuge for the oppressed, a stronghold in times of trouble. We know your name and trust you. You have never forsaken those who seek you. (Psalms 9:9, 10) We thank you that the righteous may have many troubles, but you deliver us from them all. (Psalms 34:19) We come to you, Lord, weary and burdened. Thank you for your promise to give us rest. (Matthew 11:28)
In the name of Jesus we pray,
Amen

"O Lord, be gracious to us; we long for you. Be our strength every morning, our salvation in time of distress." (Isaiah 33:2) NIV

O Lord,
 In this time of need, strengthen me. You are my strength and my shield; you are my refuge and strength, a very present help in trouble. I know, Father, that your eyes go to and fro throughout the earth to strengthen those whose hearts long for you. The body grows weary, but my hope is in you to renew my strength. I do not fear, for you are with me.
I am not dismayed or overwhelmed, for you are my God. I know you will strengthen me and help me; that you will uphold me with your righteous hand. Even as the shadows of illness cover me, I feel the comfort of your strength, Oh Lord. Thank You for your strength that carries me each day. Thank You for renewing my strength. Thank You Lord, for upholding me with your right hand. I give you the praise and the glory in the mighty name of Jesus I pray. Amen.

"All praise to the God and Father of our Lord Jesus Christ. He is the source of every mercy and the God who comforts us. He comforts us in all our troubles so that we can comfort others. When others are troubled, we will be able to give them the same comfort God has given us. You can be sure that the more we suffer for Christ, the more God will shower us with his comfort through Christ." (2 Corinthians 1:3-5) NIV

My God,

Thank you Jesus for being my comfort. How often have you noticed that soon after you receive comfort for some troubling situation, you encounter someone else facing a similar situation? It is God who leads me to these people, for the comfort I provide for them seems more credible because they know I have "been there". Paul praises the Lord in his letter to the Corinthian church that God "comforts us in all our troubles so that we can comfort others" with" the same comfort God has given us." Lord, help me to think about what Paul has said the next time I need to be comfort, or the next time I encounter someone else who needs to be comforted. Help me to always remember Lord that it is not about my problems, my situations, nor my circumstances, but rather it is all about you Lord. Let me be more willingly to share the goodness of what you have done in my life to others who are going through similar situations. Let me not be judgmental of them, but show them the love that you have showed me. Lord, forgive me for not giving the same comfort that you have given unto me to others. Forgive me if I was judgmental of any one. Lead me not into temptation but deliver me from the evil one. Lord, I love you, and adore you. I give you all the praise and the glory in the mighty name of Jesus I pray. Amen

"The earth is the Lord's and everything in it the world, and all who live in it; for he founded it upon the seas and established it upon the waters." (Psalm 24: 1-2) NIV

Lord,

You own the world and everything in it. All that I have belongs to you. Thank you, God of creation, for all the good things You've richly provided for our enjoyment - for food, clothing, and home; for godly entertainment for our children's. Help me to hold onto these things loosely, honoring you by using them for your eternal purposes. Thank you, Father, for the indescribable gift of your Son. Lord, I come to know you and your ways, I am continually grateful for all things and for every circumstance, even the difficulties you allow for my growth. I will give you thanks every day. Father, forgive me for worrying that I might not have enough to live on. I see evidence of your faithfulness all around me. I choose now to stop worrying and instead to ask for increase in my finances. Thank you for always providing exactly what I need. I resolve never to trust in wealth or to let it master me. You are my only Master, I give you the praise and the glory for all that you have done and all that you are about to do in Jesus name I pray. Amen

"Do not love the world or anything in the world. If anyone loves the world, the love of the Father is not in him. For everything in the world the cravings of sinful man, the lust of his eye and the boasting of what he has and does - comes not from the Father but from the world. The world and its desires pass away, but the man who does the will of God lives forever." (1 John 2:15-17) NIV

My God,

Thank you for giving me life more abundantly. Thank you for your word and your promises. Lord, help me to not be boastful about anything that you have blessed me, but rather to share my blessings with others so that they may be encouraged. Lord, I know that sometimes, our flesh would try to get us to get off focus of your plan for each of us, but help us to remember always that everything belongs to you. Yes, even our children, that house, the clothes that we wear, the furniture in that house, the cars that we drive, and the food that we eat. Even the money that we spend. Many a time, we have fallen short of what it is we should be doing according to your word, because our attention is on those things that we think we need in our homes, and the kind of car we should drive. But you said in your word for each of us to: Seek ye first the kingdom of heaven and all its righteousness and all these things will be added unto us." We seem to get this all mixed up, because we go after all that glory that is in the world, because we want to live like the Jones or drive like the Smiths , but I know that you also said in your word to be content in whatever state you are in. Lord, you are no concern about what's in our homes, or what type of car we drive; you want to know where our heart is. So today, I pray and ask you Lord, to created in me a pure heart, and renew the right spirit within me. Restore unto me the joy of your salvation and grant me a willing spirit, to sustain me. I love you Lord, and I give you all the glory and the honor in Jesus name I pray. Amen

"While they were eating, Jesus took bread, gave thanks and broke it, and gave it to his disciples, saying, "Take it, this is my body." Then he took the cup, gave thanks and offered it to them, and they all drank from it. "This is my blood of the covenant, which is poured out for many." (Mark 14:22-24) NIV

My God,

Thank you Jesus for the blood. Thank you for your covenant. There is a song that is song during the Lord Supper and the words are "I know it was the blood, I know it was the blood for me, one day when I was lost he died on the cross; I know it was the blood for me." In saying that this morning, we should be more grateful for that blood. Because he took many strikes for us, and his blood was shed all over the place for us. That why we need to me more thankful for Jesus and all that he went through for us. When I think about how they hit him over and over again, for what he believed in and for me, it makes me cry. Because he didn't have to do what he did for me, but he did. So, the next time you see someone that is in trouble; just remind them of his blood that was already shed for them. Let someone know that if it had not been for the blood we wouldn't be here today. Lord, I thank you for the blood. I thank you Lord for the stripes you took for me. I thank you for Jesus Christ. Lord your blood has guided me through my storms and my tribulations. Your blood has given me the strengthen I need to go on. Your blood Jesus, has molded me, shaped me, and made me to be what you would have me to be. Your blood has broken those generational curses in my families' life. Your blood has covered me each day of my life. Lord, everything I need is in your blood, glory to God. I thank you Lord, for your blood that protects me, guides me, enfolds me, strengthen me, and most of all that loves me. I thank you for all that you endure on my behalf, so that I may live for you. That's why I give you the glory and the honor today, because I love you and appreciate you. Lord, you are worthy of the praise and the glory and the honor in Jesus name I pray. Amen

"They put a purple robe on him, then twisted together a crown of thorns and set it on him. And they began to call out to him, "Hail king of the Jews!" Again and again, they struck him on the head with a staff and spit on him. And when they had mocked him, they took off the purple robe and put his own clothes on him. Then they led him out to crucify him." (Mark 15: 17-20) NIV

My Lord,

You are worthy, of all the praise and the glory. Lord, I thank you for your blood that you shed on Calvary for me. I know it was your blood that healed my body when I was sick. I know it was your blood that mended my marriage when it was falling apart. I know it was your blood that touched my finances, when I didn't have any. I know it was your blood that saved my soul. I know it was your blood that brought me out. I know it was your blood that caused the dead to rise. I know it was your blood that freed my children from the enemy. I know it was your blood that caused me to get up again. I know it was your blood that opened blond eyes. I know it was your blood that caused the deaf to hear. I know it was your blood that gave me that house. I know it was the blood that gave me that car. I know it was the blood that delivered my family and set them free. I know it was your blood that ordered my steps. I know it was your blood that protected me. I know it was your blood that gave me peace in the midst of the storm. I know it was your blood that causes my enemy to be at peace with me. I know it was your blood that spoke to my heart. I know it was your blood that brought me this far. I know it was your blood that runs in my spirit, and want let me turn around. I know it was your blood Jesus that forgave me when I sinned. Lord, I thank you for all that you endured on the cross for me. I thank you for opening my eyes to realize more and more each day that it is in the blood. Lord, help me to always remember the next time a storm comes along in my life that it is your blood that will see me through it. Therefore, I can tell the storm to move because the blood of Jesus is on it. Glory to God!

Hallelujah!!! Lord, I give you all the honor and the glory in Jesus name I pray.

"Enter his gates with thanksgiving and his courts with praise; give thanks to him and praise (bless) his name." (Psalm 100:4) NIV

Lord,

I thank you for everything You've done, everything You're doing, and everything You're going to do. I thank you for the trials and the tribulation that made me stronger. I thank you for the pain and the sorrow that made me wiser. I thank you Lord for the good and the bad that made me open my eyes wider. I thank you for the joy, because it allowed Jesus to open my heart up to give to others. I thank you Lord that I may not have must but the little that I do have I have a heart to share with others. I thank you for my home, that you allowed us to open up and invite family and friends to come together on this Thanksgiving to share in the blessings of your love. I thank you for allowing us to have food on our tables so that others can come in and break bread with us. I thank you Lord, for giving my family the love that opens the door to others to come in. I thank you that I am not a selfish person and that you have given me the ability to give back to others the love that you have given to me. I thank you Lord, for the sun, the moon, the stars, the trees, and the birds in the air. I thank you for allowing me to be content in whatever state I may be in. Lord, if I had ten thousands tongues it still will not be enough to say thank you. It is my pray that every eye that reads this prayer this day, will invite someone that they don't know to come and spend thanksgiving with their family and enjoy the food, the fun and the fellowship among God's family. It will be a good opportunity for all of us to tell them about the goodness of the Lord and maybe even get them saved. Lord, help each of us not to be selfish and ungrateful for the many blessings that you have blessed us with. It may not look like God is on your side because you maybe experiencing some hell and high water right now, but you have to remember that God will never leave you nor will he forsake you. He will not put more on you than you can bear. He is not a man that he shall lie. Every promise in the Bible shall come true if you abide by them. Have compassion on your brother or sister, forgive them, and invite them over for dinner on Thanksgiving. After all that is not your house it belongs to the Lord, he blessed you with it, but you are only the keeper of it while you here on this earth.. Because everything in heaven and earth belongs to the Lord. So quit tripping and start sharing God's house with others. God will bless you with more if you apply his principles to your household. He himself sit down and ate with tax collectors, why come you can't? Lord, I give you the praise and the glory for you along are worthy or it. I love you and I adore you in the mighty name of Jesus I pray. Amen

"I cry aloud to the Lord; I lift up my voice to the Lord for mercy. I pour out my complaint before him; before him I tell my trouble." (Psalm 142: 1-2) NIV

My Lord,

    Thank you for hearing my cry, and listening to my complaints. I thank you for all that you have done for me and what you are about to do for me, I will forever give you the glory and the praise in the mighty name of Jesus. Lord, when I am down and out I can always come to you and you listen to me without talking my business. You have always been there for me. You have strengthen me throughout all my trouble. I can't thank you for all that you have done for my family and me. You have brought us out of a many storms and many situations in each of our lives. I love you for touching the untouchable and bringing them out of all of their situations. Lord, I ask that you forgive me for always complaining about unnecessary stuff. You have opened my eyes to see those things that are important to you. You open my ears to hear what it is you are saying to me. You cleared my mind so that I can think of those things that you would have me to think about. Lord, I have so much to thank you for in my life. That is why I can give you the praise and the glory no matter what I maybe going through you have always been there for me. I put my trust in you O Lord for all the mighty works you have done in my life and in my family life. I love you and adore you in the mighty name of Jesus I pray. Amen.

"Teach me to do your will, for you are my God; may your good Spirit lead me on level ground." (Psalm 143:10) NIV

Oh Lord,

You are great, and greatly to be praise. You are the beginning and the end, my all and all. You are the author and the finisher of my life. I give you the praise and the glory. Doing the will of God begins with a total dedication of our bodies and minds. The call of God is to do two things; to offer our bodies to God, and to offer Him our minds and thus be renewed. I have two options: to be a conformer or to be a transformer. The choice is mine. With that in mind, the next principle gives me motivation for the first two. A view of God's attributes and my sinfulness compels me to offer my body and my mind to Him. With all of this in mind, I should be able to generally discern God's will for my life. God's will is known and approved through my active testing and joyful surrender. As stated in Romans 12:1-2 - "Therefore, I urge you, brothers, in view of God's mercy, to offer yourselves as living sacrifices, holy and pleasing to God - which is your spiritual worship. Do not conform any longer to the pattern of the world, but be transformed by the renewing of your mind. Then you will be able to test and approve what God's will is - good, pleasing and perfect will." This verse reveal that God's will is discovered in my action and surrender. My actions are viewing, offering, worshiping, renewing, testing, and approving. My surrender is to be living sacrifices holy and pleasing unto God. Lord, I know that your will is wise. Lord, I know that you know what is conductive to the good of your people; therefore, I surrender my will to your will for my life. I know I don't really have a choice in the matter because everything in heaven and earth belong to you; therefore, it is your will that I surrender. It is your will that I prosper and be in good health. It is your will Lord, that the favor of God surround me. It is your will Lord, that I am loaded daily with your benefits. It is your will Lord, that I love my neighbors as I love myself. It is your will that I forgive others, as you forgive me. It is your will that I help the needy and give to the poor. It is your will Lord that I feed your people. It is your will that I surrender my time, talent, and service unto you daily. It is your will that I share your word with everyone I meet. Lord, I thank you for your will in my life. I thank you for the joy of the Lord is my strength. I thank you that I am above and not beneath. I thank you for being debt free. I thank you that my marriage is set on a good foundation. I thank you that the singles are waiting on you to release a mate to them. That they are living holy and complete in you. I thank you that my children are saved, sanctified, and filled with your precious Holy Spirit. I give you all the glory and the praise in the mighty name of Jesus I pray. Amen

"Praise the LORD, all you servants of the LORD who minister by night in the house of the LORD. Lift up your hands in the sanctuary and praise the LORD. May the LORD, the Maker of heaven and earth bless you from Zion." (Psalm 134:1-3) NIV

Lord,

I will praise you all the days of my life for all the marvelous work you have done. I will praise you in the midst of my circumstances. I will praise you Lord, when trouble is all around me. I will praise you when I am sick, because my praise will heal me. I will praise you for my children being saved and delivered. I will praise you when money is funny and change is strange. I will praise you despite of all that I go through I will forever lift up my voice unto you. Because it is in my praise that I can get a breakthrough and a release from my situations or circumstances. No matter what it may look like with the nature eye, I will praise you no matter what. When praises go up blessings will come down. I will praise you until I receive my blessing of deliverance for my entire family. I will praise you until the captives are set free. I will praise you until marriages are all mended. I will praise you until I am debt free and walking in prosperity. I will praise you for my healing. I will praise you until the unemployed are employed. I will praise you until the blind can see. I will praise you until the deaf can hear. I will praise you for the joy of the Lord is my strength. I will bless your holy name forever. You along are worthy of all the praise and the glory in the mighty name of Jesus I pray. Amen

"I wait for the Lord, my soul waits, and in his word I put my hope. My soul waits for the Lord more than watchmen wait for the morning, more than watchmen wait for the morning." (Psalm 130:5-6) NIV

My God,

   Thank you that waiting time is not wasted time; it is just a matter of time. I will wait on you Lord for my hope is in you and not in man. I will wait upon my finances so that I can walk in prosperity. I will wait upon you Lord for deliverance of my family members. I will wait upon you Lord for salvation for each family member. I will wait upon you Lord to lead me in the right direction. I will wait upon you Father, for the blessings that you have in store for me. I will wait on you Lord because they that wait upon the Lord shall renew their strength. I will wait upon you Lord, to stir up the gifts in me. I will wait upon you for my healing. I will wait upon you for that new house. I will wait upon you Lord, for that new car. I will wait upon you Lord, to renew my joy. I will wait upon you Lord to restore me, in all areas of my life. I will wait upon you Lord to order my steps and direct my pathway. I will wait upon you Lord to give me favor on my job, in my church, in my community, and in my home. I will wait upon you because my hope will always be in you. Lord, I love you and I praise you in the mighty name of Jesus I pray. Amen

"O house of Israel, trust in the Lord - he is their help and shield. O house of Aaron, trust in the Lord - he is their help and shield, You who fear him, trust in the Lord - he is their help and shield." (Psalm 115; 9-11) NIV

Oh Lord,

Thank you for being my shield and my helper. Thank you for shielding me from the enemy. Thank you for helping me when I was down and out. Thank you Lord for your grace and your mercy. Thank you for fresh new manna that you pour out fresh and new each day. Thank you for the joy that I feel deep down in my soul. Thank you that nothing else matters to me. Thank you for hope. Thank you Lord for being my Father, my friend, and my comforter. Thank you for all that you have done, and all that you are about to do. Thank you for moving obstacles and people out of my pathway so that I can see you. Thank you Lord, for your word and your promises. Thank you for your hands being upon me, and keeping me from pain. Thank you for enlarging my territory. Thank you Father, for your goodness and your mercy. Thank you for being the joy of my life. I give you the praise and the glory forever and forever in Jesus name. Amen

"He sends forth His word and heals them and rescues them from the pit and destruction." (Psalm 107:20) NIV

My Father who art in heaven, hallowed be thy name,

      Lord, I come this morning to give you the glory and the honor and the praise for truly you have been good to all of us. You have been better to us than we have been to ourselves. You are Alpha and Omega, the Beginning and the End. You are the author and the finisher of our faith. That's why we can come boldly to your throne of grace and mercy and ask what we will in your Son name and we shall receive it. Lord, someone somewhere today is feeling rejected. The pain of emotional rejection is one of the worst kinds of pain a person can feel. When a person feels he has been rejected, there is intense emotional pain. It hurts! We need to always remember to check our perception when one is feeling rejected. Just because you feel rejected or perceive rejection does not mean you are really being rejected. It may be the result of past problems, and, if so, it is time to receive healing through the word of God. Because God said in his word that he would never leave you nor forsake you. He will be with you even until the end. He will make a way out of no way for you. He will guide you into all righteousness for his namesake. He said yea though we walk through the valley of the shadow of death he will be with us. His rod and his staff comfort us. Nay, in all these things we are more than conquerors through him that loved us. He loved us so much that he gave his only Son up for us to have eternal life. Now that alone is awesome and something to always shouts about. Lord, our Father, I thank you for all that you have done, all that you are about to do, and all that you are going to do for us. I thank you that you have lifted the spirit of rejection from my brother/sisters heart and spirit. I thank you that you have molded them and shaped them to be what you would have them to be and not what man would say they are. I thank you that they are mighty men and women of God walking in your anointing and integrity of the word of God. I thank you that you have ordered their footsteps, and directed their pathway. I thank you for you are worthy of the glory and the honor. Now Lord, forgive us for all sins, and lead us not into temptation but deliver us from the evil one. For thine is the kingdom, the power, and the glory forever and ever. In Jesus name, I pray Amen

"Thy word is a lamp unto my feet, and a light unto my path" (Psalm 119:105) NIV

Heavenly Father,

Lord, I thank you for your word being a light unto my pathway. I thank you that your word has opened doors for me that man could not open. I thank you Father, that your word has healed me. I thank you that your word has been my shelter in times of trouble. I thank you Lord, that your word has been my rock in difficult situations. I thank you that your word has changed my family member's life and mines as well. I thank you that your word has turned my life around and set me upon a solid rock. I thank you that I can stand firmly upon your word and not be move able. But always abiding in your word. I thank you Lord, that your word is my strength. I thank you that your word Lord is my joy. I thank you that your word is my peace in times of trouble. I thank you that your word gives me grace and mercy. I thank you that your word will forever be my shield and my protection. I thank you that your word will give me favor. I thank you that your word healed broken marriages, and destroys the yoke of the enemy. I thank you Lord that your word will turn the heart of every non-believer to believe. I thank you that your word will not return unto you void but it will accomplish what it set out to accomplish in the name of Jesus. Your word gives me joy when I am down. Your word gives me strength when I am weak. Your word gives me power to tell that problem, situation or circumstance to be removed and cast into the sea. I thank you that your word Lord, lights up my footstep so that I can see how to walk in your word. Lord, I want your word to always to guide me, and lead me into the areas of ministry that you sent me and not man. I want your word to be my light and my strength forever. I know Lord, that without your word in my life, I cannot do anything, but with it in my life; I can do all things through Christ Jesus who strengthen me. I give you all the honor and the glory for your word and your promises for this walk of life and the life to come in Jesus name I pray. Amen

"Come to me, all you who are weary and burdened, and I will give you rest. Take my yoke upon you and learn from me, for I am gentle and humble in heart, and you will find rest for your souls. For my yoke is easy and my burden is light." (Matthew 11:28-30) NIV

Oh Lord,

    Thank you for giving me rest and taken the burden off me. Lord, I know that sometimes in my walk, I will become weary and restless but I have to remind myself that this burden is not mine it is yours. I come this morning Lord to lift up every hindering burden off my shoulder and give it all over to you. Lord, I lift my home and bills up to you. I lift my children and grandchildren up to you. I lift up my finances up to you. I lift up my job situations up to you. I lift up my heart and my soul up to you to mend and renew as you see fit. I lift up my aches and pains up to you. I lift up my marriages and my spouse up to you. I lift up my family members the saved and unsaved up to you. I lift up my church family up to you. I lift my Pastor and all his problems and situations concerning the church up to you. I lift up the burden that he may have concerning the ministry to you Lord. I ask right now Lord that you lift any burden from him in the name of Jesus. I ask that total deliverance take place in each of my family member's life right now in the name of Jesus. I pray for release and dismissal of every case that has been brought against them in the name of Jesus. Satan, I come to serve you final notice that my family and my church family life's are set upon the solid rock that the Lord Jesus has established before them and that their minds, souls, and spirit belongs to God. He is the head of their life; He rules and abides in their spirit man as well as in my spirit man and my soul. You are no long welcome or needed in this family of believers so I send you back to the pit of hell from whence you cometh from in the name of Jesus. Thank you Lord for saving and delivering my family and my church family from any bondages and setting them free in the name of Jesus. I thank you for your love and your patience. I thank you that you are a forgiving God. Thank you for your mercy and your grace. I give you all the praise and the glory in the mighty name of Jesus I do pray. Amen.

"So he went to Zarephath. When he came to the town gate, a widow was there gathering sticks. He called to her and asked, "Would you bring me a little water in a jar so I may have a drink?" As she was going to get it, he called, "And bring me, please, a piece of bread." "As surely as the Lord your God lives," she replied, "I don't have any bread, only a handful of flour in a jar and a little oil in a jug. I am gathering a few sticks to take home and make a meal for myself and my son that we may eat it and die." (I Kings 17:10-12) NIV

My Lord,

Teach us how to give cheerfully to all we met or come into contact with. It's doesn't matter what they are going to do with what we give as long as we give from our heart, and we give because you told us to give. Many times, we give and expect a return from it. That is not what you want us to do, because if we give to someone who is in need and do it from our heart then and only then will you bless us. We think that giving is always monetary giving, but we can give in our time and in our talents. If God has given you the talent to sew, or teach then you should give that talent back unto the kingdom of God do something productive in your church. It would help the kingdom of God to grow. If God has given you the talent to do computer work (secretary work, receptionist work etc...) give that talent back to God and allow Him to bless you through it. The Bible tell us that we should work while it is day, because when night cometh no man can work. Why not work for God in the kingdom and allow your blessing to overflow. This widow in the scripture gave all that she had to Elijah, and the craziest think about it all is that she did not really know him at all. But she gave without complaining, not grudgingly, without hesitation. She gave from her heart. Thinking this was going to be her last meal on the earth. But nevertheless, God showed up and the Bible says that she never ran out of flour and oil. So, you see in God's economy we cannot afford not to give if we want to be blessed and be a blessing to someone else. Lord, help us to give from the heart and not from the flesh. Help us to give more unto your kingdom in the area of tithes, offering, talents, and our time. Help us Father, to be obedient to your word, because you said you love a cheerful giver. You also said, that when we give it would be given back to us, good measures, pressed down, shaken together, and running over will men give unto our bosom. Thank you Lord, for blessing me in the area of giving to others, and to your kingdom. Use me Lord, to help build up your kingdom. In the name of Jesus, I pray. Amen

"The angel of the Lord encamps around those who fear him, and he delivers them." (Psalm 34:7) NIV

"GOD's angel sets up a circle of protection around us while we pray." (Psalm 34:7) The Message Bible

My God,

Thank you for encamping your angel around me so that nothing will harm me. Lord, when I think of how you kept me from many seen and unseen I just want to say thank you. I know that when I enter into your throne room of prayer you are surrounding me and keeping me from all danger and evil. When I enter into my closet for prayer you are with me and no good things will you withhold from me. Lord, when I needed a friend you were there. When I was sick, you healed me. When I was going through the many obstacles, you were by my side. When my so-called friends turned there back on me, you were my friend. When my children were not acting right, you touched them. Lord, when I needed shelter you gave me a home. When I need transportation, you gave me a car. When I needed my bills paid, you made a way out of no way. All of this was to let me know that you Lord, have continually encamped your angels around me whenever I needed to be protected. That why I can say over and over again Lord, I thank you and I love you. I give you all the praise and the glory for your angels that watch over and protect me. Because I know that when I enter into the throne room and I begin to press my way into the Holy of Hollies you have charged your angel to protect me while I pray. Many times when I go into prayer and I go behind the veil to intercede for someone my body, my finances will come under attack after I finish. But it is good to know that the weapons will form but they will not prosper because you are with me. You have my back through it all. Lord, you are so good. I love you and adore you and your praises will always be in my mouth. I give you the glory and the honor in Jesus name I pray. Amen

"Give and it will be given to you. A good measure, pressed down, shaken together and running over, will be poured into your lap. For with the measure you use, it will be measured to you." (Luke 6:38 NIV)

"Give away your life; you'll find life given back, but not merely given back—given back with bonus and blessing. Giving, not getting is the way. Generosity begets generosity." (Luke 6:38 Message)

My God,

Giving does not always have to be money; God wants our time, as well. God you gave me your word and you're only begotten Son. All I have to do is apply your word to my life so that I may live eternally. When I think of the word **give** and the acronym for the word, it brings joy to my soul. Because God showed me this sometime ago that the very word GIVE means **G= God, I=Is, V=victorious, E= every time**. Which simply means when we give our time, our money, and our talents unto the kingdom, that God will be victorious in our situation every time. No matter what we are going through God will get the glory every time. The next time you get ready to give think about the problem and tell God, I know that I maybe going through in this area but I know that my giving is a direct result of you being victorious in it. Then give God some praise for it. It maybe that the seed you sowed is for your children, your marriage, your finances, your home, your car, maybe even for a family member who is in prison, whatever it is give and God will show up and show out in that very situation. Give cheerfully whatever you give, give from your heart and not from your flesh. Because God honors a cheerful giver. Lord, I thank you for allowing me to give my money, my talents, my life, and my children to do the work of the kingdom. I know Lord that many people may not understand why I spend so much time and energy working at your kingdom, but that's okay too. Because I know that working for the Lord will pay off after while. Lord, you gave each of us your Son so that we may live a life eternal. So why shouldn't we give you all that we have so that we can be blessed abundantly. Thank you Lord for loving me so much that you gave me your word to life by daily. Thank You Lord that you love me that you gave me your Son. Thank you Lord for loving me that you guide me through each day's situations. That's' why I can always give you the praise and the glory for your love unconditional. I love you and I adore you in Jesus name I pray. Amen.

"Create in me a pure heart, O God, and renew a steadfast spirit within me. Do not cast me from your presence or take your Holy Spirit from me. Restore to me the joy of your salvation and grant me a willing spirit, to sustain me." (Psalm 51:10-12) NIV

"God, make a fresh start in me, shape a Genesis week from the chaos of my life. Don't throw me out with the trash, or fail to breathe holiness in me. Bring me back from gray exile; put a fresh wind in my sails!" (Psalm 51:10-12) Message

My God,

Touch my heart Lord, I have been wounded in the church, in my home, on my job, and in my relationships with my brothers/sister. The pain is so real that it is unbearable. It feels like a knife has been place in my heart and it is turning and turning. Oh Lord, touch my heart, and let me not harden my heart to this pain. Give me a new heart Lord. Create in me a heart of servitude. A heart like yours. A heart that will turn the other cheek. A heart that will love unconditional. A heart that will have compassion for my brothers/sisters. A heart that will obey your word. Lord, give me a clean heart. One that is white as snow and without sin. My joy Lord, I need more joy in my life so that I can enjoy the salvation that you have given me. Lord, please don't turn your back on me. I want to live right. I want to do right. I want to have joy abundantly. Lord, I need you in my life. I need to know Lord that everything will be okay. I need to know that no matter what I may go through you will be there to pick me up. Lord, I need your help to live a life holy and complete in you. I need your help Lord, to forgive my brothers/sisters of all past hurt and pain. Lord, I need your word to live in me daily so that I will not sin against you. I need to hear a word from you Lord. Please remove that knife from my heart so that I may live. That's it Lord, I feel it being remove and I feel your presences in my heart. It feels so good and so warm. Thank you for not allowing me to die at the hand of my enemy. Thank you for renewing and restoring my soul and my joy. I feel it now Lord, your presences in my heart. I love you Lord. Yes, I will do your will. Yes, I will obey. Yes Lord, I will go. Thank you for being my Father, my friend, and my Lord and Savior. I give you all the praise, the glory, and the honor for renewing my soul unto you. In Jesus name, I pray. Amen

"For the mouth speaks out of that which fills the heart." (Matthew 12:34)NASB

"You brood of vipers, how can you who are evil say anything good? For out of the overflow of the heart the mouth speaks." (Matthew 12:34) NIV

"You have minds like a snake pit! How do you suppose what you say is worth anything when you are so foul-minded? It is your heart, not the dictionary that gives meaning to your words. A good person produces good deeds and words season after season. An evil person is blight on the orchard. Let me tell you something: Every one of these careless words is going to come back to haunt you. There will be a time of Reckoning. Words are powerful; take them seriously. Words can be your salvation. Words can also be your damnation." (Matthew 12:34-37)Message Bible

My Lord,

Life and death is in the power of our tongue. With my tongue, I can choose to speak good things or negative things about my situation and about my life. I have to stop talking about my life situation and struggles as if they are never going to go away. My problems rather it is big or small is a matter of what I say about them and to whom I say them. When I speak about them to the Lord, I should never speak about it again. Because that means that, I am not allowing God to work it out or solve it. My mind affects what I say through my mouth, and my mouth affects my mind. It is very difficult for me to stop speaking of my situation until I stop thinking about it. Lord, today I give all my thoughts, my words that I speak to you, so that you can solve them and fix them. I speak healing over my body. I speak debt cancellation over my finances. I speak deliverance, sanctification over all of my family members. I speak joy unspeakable joy over my family. I speak new car, new homes and new attitudes over my friends. I speak peace over the nation of Israel. I speak to every cancer patient body, that cancer cell be dissolved in the name of Jesus. I speak to every heart disease in the name of Jesus, your bloodline must line up with the word of God. Lord, make every crooked or blood artery to line up and flow correctly in the name of Jesus. I speak to those dry bones in every person body this morning, straight out and line up with the word of God. The Lord is the strength of my blood line, my artery, my heart, my veins, my eyesight, my hearing, my speech, my backbone, my feet, my knees, my hands, my fingers, my toes, and my whole body from the inside out, therefore everything in me must line up with what the word of God says. Lord, I thank you for touching me this morning and giving me divine revelation of your word today to apply to my life in the mighty name of Jesus I pray. Amen

" Not that I have already obtained all this, or have already been made perfect, but I press on to take hold of that for which Christ Jesus took hold of me. Brothers, I do not consider myself yet to have taken hold of it. But one thing I do; forgetting what is behind and straining toward what is ahead. I press on toward the goal to win the prize for which God has called me heavenward in Christ Jesus." (Philippians 3:12-14) NIV

"I'm not saying that I have this all together, that I have it made. But I am well on my way, reaching out for Christ, who has so wondrously reached out for me. Friends, don't get me wrong: By no means do I count myself an expert in all of this, but I've got my eye on the goal, where God is beckoning us onward—to Jesus. I'm off and running and I'm not turning back." (Philippians 3:12-14) Message Bible

My God,

I love reading the Message Bible because it breaks it down so that even a small child can understand it. Many of us today are worry and concern about things that are in our past and not focusing on what is ahead of us. Today I just believe God is telling each of us to keep our eyes focus on the goal to which he is calling each of us. You maybe called to be an evangelist, a pastor, a teacher, a missionary, a prayer warrior, or an intercessor, whatever God has called you to do it wholeheartedly as unto the Lord. The Lord is looking for true worshipers and praisers to help build his kingdom and to help take it to another level in him. So, we must get about our Father's business. God will not ask you to do something if he didn't equip you to do it. He has given each of us the power to call those things that be not as if they were. He will bring you to it and through it. No matter how hard and difficult the task may seem, he will bring you through it. So what no one wants to show up to prayer, you show up because the word of God says where **one** or two are gather in his name there he will be in the midst. We have to stop worry about what other people are doing and do what God has called us to do. After all, we can't get anyone in heaven but our self.

Lord, I thank you for giving me the opportunity to email this prayer to your people this morning that it might encourage, strength, and motivate someone in their walk with you. I give you all the glory and the honor for this ministry, you have birth in me. Lord, let every eye that read this email be bless and encouraged to press on toward their goal in Christ Jesus. Lord, if we all would take the time to search our heart and minds and to ask you to make us over again we will be the men and women of God that you have ordained us to be. Lord, help us to move forward in your word and in your anointing that we don't have the time nor the energy to waste on what someone else is not doing and what they are doing, but what is going on in the spiritual ream with us. Forgive us Lord for being judge- mental, or critical of one another. Forgive us Lord, for not being obedient to what you have called us to do or say. Forgive us Lord, for any sins that we may have committed. Lord, I give you the praise and the glory as well as the honor for everything you are doing in the life of your people in Jesus name I pray. Amen

"Jabez was more honorable than his brothers. His mother had named him Jabez, saying, "I gave birth to him in pain." Jabez cried out to the God of Israel, "Oh that you would bless me and enlarge my territory! Let your hand be with me, and keep me from harm so that I will be free from pain." And God granted his request." (I Chronicles 4:9-10) NIV

"Jabez was a better man than his brothers, a man of honor. His mother had named him Jabez (Oh, the pain!), saying, "A painful birth! I bore him in great pain!" Jabez prayed to the God of Israel: "Bless me, O bless me! Give me land, large tracts of land. And provide your personal protection—don't let evil hurt me." God gave him what he asked." (I Chronicles 4: 9-10) Message Bible

My God,

We all go through hard aches and pains in our lifetimes. Some more than others. But nevertheless, we have to realize that it is through those birthing pain that God will show up and show out in our life. The pain may even seem hard like a woman going through birthing pain. But when we call on Jesus to protect up and to guide us through those pains, we are strong through it all. The Bible said that Jabez called on the Lord in prayer, and asks God to bless him, and to enlarge his territory. Many of us are trying to bear that burden alone and we need to call on the God of Israel as well. Because when we call upon the name of Jesus he will heal us, he will strengthen us, he will protect us, he will guide us, and he will lead us in the right direction. God wants us to call upon him and to kneel in prayer to him. He told us to pray without ceasing. Not to just pray when we need something or going through something, but to pray and trust him for everything. When we go down on our knees to pray and ask God to enlarge our territory that could mean alot of things. I know when I go down and I ask God to enlarge my territory in all areas of my life. That means, I am asking him to enlarge my finances, my health (let it be good health), my marriage, my children, my home my car I drive, my family and friends, and everything or anything else that needs to be enlarged by what the word of God says about it. I ask Him to grant me a willing heart and a determination to serve him wholeheartedly. Not to allow my foot to slip nor my mouth to become negative in anything I do for Him. I want all of what God has for me. Therefore, I must be willing to do his will and not mine. Lord, I love you and I thank you for enlarging my territory. I thank you that I am blessed going in and blessed coming out. I am blessed because I serve a mighty God. I am blessed because the Lord has made me in His own image and I am a child of his. Lord, I thank you and I give you the praise and the glory for all that you do and all that you are about to do in my life. In Jesus name, I pray. Amen.

"A man of many companions may come to ruin, but there is a friend who sticks closer than a brother." (Proverbs 18:24) NIV

"Friends come and friends go, but a true friend sticks by you like family." (Proverbs 18:24) Message Bible

My Lord,

Thank you for being a friend to the friendless. Thank you for being a friend to me. When I was down and out, you were there for me. When I needed a shoulder to cry on you were there. When I needed a hand to hold, you gave me yours. When I was going through the loss of a love one, you were there to comfort me. When I was sick, you were there to heal me and touch me with your power. When I was down and out, you picked me up. When I needed shelter, there you were. When I needed someone to talk to you were there to listen to me. Lord, you have been a friend to me. You have stuck by me when no one else has. You have protected me, when I needed protection. Thank you for covering me with your blood and crowning my head with wisdom and knowledge of your word. With you on my side, I don't need anyone else. Lord, many of people have walked into my life as a friend, and many of them remain and many of them are no longer there. Some said they were my friend but where were they when I needed them the most, not there. Because a true friend will be, there no matter what they are going through. I thank you Lord, that I can call you a friend. I thank you that I am a friend of God. Now, Lord, I pray for all of those who say they are friends to someone and are not. I ask in the name of Jesus that they first get a true relationship with you and allow you to become there friend. Then I ask that they learn how to love themselves as a friend. Let them know Lord, that friend keeps secrets, and pray for each other and it's not just a one sided prayers. A true friend will make sure your needs are met before theirs are met. There isn't a better friend like Jesus. Lord, I give you the praise and the glory for being a friend of mine and for loving me unconditional. In Jesus name, I pray. Amen

"Am I now trying to win the approval of men, or of God? Or am I trying to please men? If I were still trying to please men, I would not be a servant of Christ." (Galatians 1:10) NIV

"Do you think I speak this strongly in order to manipulate crowds? Or curry favor with God? Or get popular applause? If my goal was popularity, I wouldn't bother being Christ's slave." (Galatians 1:10) Message Bible

My God,

Oh my God, what is wrong with me that I must try to get applause from man for what I do? That is not of you. Many of us are guilty of this, and some of us would not own up to even doing it. But I thank God that only what I do for Christ will last. I must work for the Lord each day so that I may get approval from him. The only way that I can please God is to have faith and to be obedient to His word. I must obey God even if it may cost me my reputation and my friends. So what they are talking about me. So what they are being judgmental of me. So what they are marking me. I thank God that they are, because that put me in the list with God, because people talk about him everyday. He was being judged by people, and he had people marking what he did. Lord, if I lost friends over my stand with you and doing your will oh well that means they were not my friends in the first place. So move them out of my path way and replace them with true friends that want to see me go higher and higher in your word and in your anointing. Replace them with friends that will encourage me and lift me up and will walk with me in the ministry that you have ordained for me. Lord, let me not be a people pleaser, but rather a God pleaser in everything that I do and say. Because I know that people don't have a heaven nor a hell to put me in, but you God have the last say as to where I will live eternity. Lord, surround me with true godly people, who know you and are living their life for you. So, Lord, let me be ready when you call my name, and lead me into my final resting place. Father, I thank you for leading me and guiding me and keeping me saved, sanctified, and full of your Holy Spirit in the name of Jesus Christ I pray. Amen

"When you fast, do not look somber as the hypocrites do, for they disfigure their faces to show men they are fasting. I tell you the truth; they have received their reward in full. But when you fast, put oil on your head and wash your face, so that it will not be obvious to men that you are fasting, but only to your Father, who is unseen; and your Father, who sees what is done in secret, will reward you." (Matthew 6:16-18) NIV

"When you practice some appetite-denying discipline to better concentrate on God, don't make a production out of it. It might turn you into a small-time celebrity but it won't make you a saint. If you 'go into training' inwardly, act normal outwardly. Shampoo and comb your hair, brush your teeth, wash your face. God doesn't require attention-getting devices. He won't overlook what you are doing; he'll reward you well." (Matthew 6:16-18) Message Bible

My God,

Thank you Jesus, for this awesome word of wisdom this morning. Many of us who go on fast like to tell everyone that is around us that we are fasting. But your word tells us that our fasting should only be between you and the person who is called to fast. The reason we fast is simply to get to another level in you, and to have more wisdom and knowledge instilled in us through our obedient to your word and studying the word daily. Fasting is an ultimate sacrifice that we give to God. Whatever God has called you to fast from that is what you need to do. If God brings you to a fast, he will bring you through it. Lord, I pray that you would sustain me and everyone that is reading this as they seek you for a godly fast or whatever it is that you have called them to fast for. Let your words be the only thing that we eat, sleep and think about daily. Cover me Lord with your blood, and giving me a willing and determinate heart to serve you more and more each day. Let you're good and perfect will be done in my life, in my family, and in the life of everyone that I come in contact with this day. Let the words of my mouth and the meditation of my heart be acceptable in thy sight O Lord, my

Savior and Redeemer. Order my steps in your word. Lead me and guide me every day. Let your anointing fall on me as I strive to do your will. Let this old flesh of mine die and let your word and your anointing increase in my life. Lord, I thank you and I praise you once more and again for all that you have done and all that you are about to do in the life of your people through fasting and praying. In the mighty name of Jesus, I pray. Amen.

"So in everything do to others what you would have them do to you, for this sums up the Law and the Prophets." (Matthew 7:12) NIV

"Here is a simple, rule-of-thumb guide for behavior: Ask yourself what you want people to do for you, then grab the initiative and do it for them. Add up God's Law and Prophets and this is what you get." (Matthew 7:12) Message Bible

Oh Lord,

Guilty as charged. There have been many times that I was not nice to someone, or I may have said something unkind to them. We all are guilty of not treating others as we would treat ourselves. Lord, I ask in the name of Jesus that you help me to treat my family and friends the same way I want to be treated. If I want to be loved, I have to show love to them. If I want them to have compassion for me, I have to have compassion for them. If I want them to forgive my faults and sins, then I need to forgive them as well. If I want them to respect me, I have to respect them as well. If I want them to give to me, I have to be willing to give unto them as well. Lord, I know that this walk of life is not an easy task, but I also know that if I want to be like you I have to live by the word of God. So, today Father, I ask that you first and foremost forgive me for being selfish, prideful, hateful at times, and unlovable. I ask that you forgive me Father, for not always showing compassion and love unto everyone that needs it. I ask that you Father, forgive me if I have allow others to use my ear as a garage can for there gossip. I don't want anything Lord to go in my ear canal but the word of God, because what goes in must come out. So, I ask today Lord, that you make me over from the inside out. That you Lord, mold me and shape me to be that man or woman of God that you have ordained for me to be. Let this flesh die this day so that I may live a life holy and complete in your and in your word. Lord, I thank you for what you are doing in my life. I give you the praise and the glory in Jesus name I pray. Amen

"How good and pleasant it is when brothers live together in unity! It like precious oil poured on the head, running down on the beard, running down on Aaron's beard, down upon the collar of his robes. It is as if the dew of Hermon were falling on Mount Zion. For there the LORD bestows his blessing, even life forevermore." (Psalm 133) NIV

"How wonderful, how beautiful, when brothers and sisters get along! It's like costly anointing oil flowing down head and beard, flowing down Aaron's beard, flowing down the collar of his priestly robes. It's like the dew on Mount Hermon flowing down the slopes of Zion. Yes, that's where God commands the blessing, ordains eternal life." (Psalm 133) Message Bible

My God,

Oh how wonderful, how beautiful it is when brothers and sisters get along together in the spirit of love. It's like music to your ears. When we can come together and forget about our problems, our situations and fellowship in harmony with one another. Oh when that day comes when we can sing and shout unto the Lord a new song. When we as brothers and sisters can feel the pain of one another and intercede on behalf of one another. Lord, let your will be done so that we can be the children's you have called each of us to be. Help us to realize that we come this far by faith, trusting in your holy name and we can't turn around. Lord, we should be able to get along better with one another because there is no big you or little I in this relationship we should have with you and with one another. But, Lord, many of times we find ourselves in a battle with one another. Trying to out do each other. Who has the biggest car, or house. Who has the most anointing? Who has the best job? Who has the perfect children? Who can sing better? Who can preach or teach the loudest. Who makes the most money? It's always something with my brothers and sisters. Lord, I know that you told me to be content in whatever state I am in. Whether it be my car breaking down, my home is not a house, my children giving me problems, my unemployment, my not having what I need to pay my bills, whatever it is I am content. I can't complain because you have been too good to my family and me. You have brought us a mighty long way. We are forever grateful for the small and the big things that you do for us. That's why Lord, I can give you the praise and the glory for all that you do, all that you are about to do, and everything that you have done in my life. I love you and I adore you, and I glorify your name. Thank you Lord, for the attitude of gratitude that you have giving me. Thank you for your love, your patience, and your kindness in Jesus name I pray. Amen

"Praise the LORD, all you servants of the LORD who minister by night in the house of the LORD. Lift up your hands in the sanctuary and praise the LORD. May the LORD, the Maker of heaven and earth, bless you from Zion." (Psalm 134) NIV

"Come; bless God, all you servants of God! You priests of God, posted to the night watch in God's shrine, Lift your praising hands to the Holy Place, and bless God. In turn, may God of Zion bless you—God who made heaven and earth!" (Psalm 134) Message Bible

Oh God,

How excellent is your name. You are worthy of glory and honor. You are my rock and my shield, my protector. You made me in your image. You are great and greatly to be praise. You are my all and all. Lord, I don't see why someone wouldn't praise your name. You made each of us. You molded us and shaped us to be what we are today. You have blessed us to have life and have it more abundantly. You are the creator of everything. That along is a reason to give you the praise and the glory. I don't understand Lord, how someone can be in church and not lift up there hands to give you the praise. They act as if you haven't done anything at all for them. It was there alarm clock that woke them up. It was there mind that told them to put that dress or suit on. It was there friends that brought them out of sin. The devil is a lie. It has always been you and you along have done all this for us and you will continue to do it for us. You have done so much for me that I can't help but to give you the praise and the glory. I will praise you in the sanctuary. I will praise you in my home, on my job. I will praise you in the grocery store. I will praise you in my car. I will praise you everywhere I go. I will exalt your holy name. That's why I lift my hands to you in total gratitude. You said in your word that if you be lifted up you would draw all men unto you. Lord, I lift you up I magnify your name. You are worthy. I love you and I adore you. I can tell you enough how much I love you and I am grateful for all that you do and all that you are about to do in my life. In the name of Jesus, I pray. Amen.

"O God, you are my God, earnestly I seek you; my soul thirsts for you, my body longs for you, in a dry and weary land where there is no water. I have seen you in the sanctuary and beheld your power and your glory. Because your love is better than life, my lips will glorify you. I will praise you as long as I live, and in your name I will lift up my hands." (Psalm 63:1-4) NIV

"God—you're my God! I can't get enough of you! I've worked up such hunger and thirst for God, traveling across dry and weary deserts. So here, I am in the place of worship, eyes open, drinking in your strength and glory. In your generous love, I am really living at last! My lips brim praises like fountains. I bless you every time I take a breath; my arms wave like banners of praise to you." (Psalm 63:1-14) Message Bible

Oh Lord,

How wonderful is your name, you reign in heaven and in earth. Lord, I will praise your holy name forever and ever. No matter what I maybe going through right now, I will still give your name the praise and the glory. Because I know that, you are the one who will bring me through my present circumstances and situation. That's why I will give you the praise. I will lift up my hands to exalt you. I will praise you in the midst of my storm. I will praise you and exalt you when I am sick. I will praise you when I am broke and can't pay my bills. I will praise you when my children are acting up. I will praise you in the sanctuary. I will praise you in my car. I will praise you in my home. I will praise you on my job. I will praise you everywhere I go. I will give you all the praise in the morning, in the afternoon, and in the evening. I will praise you because I love you. I will praise you O Lord, because of what you have done for me. I will praise you for bringing me out of darkness into the marvelous light. I will praise you because you are my friend, my mother, my father, and my all and all. Thank you for being my all and all. Thank you for loving me enough to forgive me of my sins. I love you and adore you and I give you my total praise in Jesus name I pray. Amen.

"Keep on loving each others as brothers. Do not forget to entertain strangers, for by so doing some people have entertained angels without knowing it." (Hebrews 13:2) NIV

"Stay on good terms with each other, held together by love. Be ready with a meal or a bed when it's needed. Why, some have extended hospitality to angels without ever knowing it." (Hebrews 13:1-2) Message Bible

Oh my God,

    Lord, we are all guilty of mistreating someone or somebody. Rather it be in our family or on our jobs, or even in our church. We have talked about them in a bad way. We have judged them by what they wear, or what they say. We have turned our back on them when they needed us the most. We have been rude to them. We even have made the statement that we don't like them sometime or another. We judge them by the clothes they wear, the way they wear their hair, the color of there skin, or even how they talk. We have been rude in our conversation with them. We haven't showed love to them, but rather hatred. We have not showed the God kind of respect for them. We have not even showed that brotherly love that we are supposed to show one another. Lord, we say we are a Christian, but yet we don't act like a Christian. We act like the world. We thought we had changed but our flesh keeps us in the sin nature that we are in. Simply because we have not learn how to totally surrender our all and all to you. Help each of us today Lord, to live a life of what we preach and talk about daily. Help us, not to hold a grudge, but to love unconditional. Help us, Father, to show respect for one another. Help us Lord, to get about your business, because when we are about your business we don't have time to get into somebody else business. Help us Lord, to give to the poor, and to love on them despite of what they are going through. We all go through something. Help us not to judge them by what they don't have. Instead let us help them to get what they need. Lord, I pray and ask that you use me as a worthy vessel to help those who need a word from you and to love on them with the God kind of love. Lord, speak to the heart of all your children so that we all can be on one accord with what the word of God says. Don't allow us to lean to the left or the right, but make every crocked edge straight in our life. Lord, I thank you for using me to be a worthy vessel in this time of trials and tribulation that we all are going through. I thank you that you spoke to my heart concerning these prayers. Now Lord, I ask that every person who reads this prayer will surrender his/her all and all to you in a great way. I love you and adore you Lord and I will continue to give you the praise and the glory in Jesus name I pray. Amen.

"For <u>God</u> did <u>not give</u> us a <u>spirit</u> of timidity (fear), but a <u>spirit of</u> <u>power, of love and of self-discipline</u>." (II Timothy 1:7) NIV

"And the special gift of ministry you received when I laid hands on you and prayed—keep that ablaze! God doesn't want us to be shy with his gifts, but bold and loving and sensible." (II Timothy 1:7) Message Bible

My God,

You have called me to do a great work for you and through you. Therefore, I can't allow Satan and his team to take me off focus of that which you have called me to do. I can't allow fear, spirit of doubting, the spirit of unbelief to come into play in this matter. Lord, many of us have been called to do something for you but because of fear, and doubting we just sit on it and not move on it. We as children of God need to stop allowing the spirit of fear to rule in our life and begin to activate the spirit of I can do all things through Christ Jesus who strength me to rule in our heart and our mind. We are a chosen generation, a royal priesthood, and because of that we have the authority to do all that God has ordained us to do. If he brings you to it, trust him to bring you through it. He will never put more on you than you can bear. He is a God just like that. When we least expect it, he will open up a door for each of us to walk right into our calling or our gifts. So my brother /sister what ever it is that you know that God has called you to do, quit sitting on it and begin to move on it. This maybe your season of blessings. You maybe were getting ready to walk in your destiny. The Lord will not call you to do something without not giving you the provision to do it. So, quit worry, quit doubting, and quit fearing what you don't know yet. Walk in it, just do it. Lord, I thank you for the call that you have placed over my life. I thank you for the gifts that you have bestowed upon me. Now Lord, I ask that you use me for you kingdom building, let my flesh die completely, and let your will be done in my life right now in the name of Jesus I pray. Amen

"Now faith is being sure of what we hope for and certain of what we do not see This is what the ancients were commended for." (Hebrews 11:1-2) NIV

"The fundamental fact of existence is that this trust in God, this faith, is the firm foundation under everything that makes life worth living. It's our handle on what we can't see. The act of faith is what distinguished our ancestors, set them above the crowd." (Hebrews 11:1-2) Message Bible

My God,

I come this morning walking by faith and not by sight. Asking whatever I will in your name knowing that I shall receive it. Lord, sometimes, my spirit is troubled with the things of this world. I seem to want the very best for everyone, but yet, I forget about myself. I seem to ask all the time that you bless my family and friends, and never myself. I know that is what you would have me to do. But Lord, I am tired and I have needs as well as the next person. We all have felt this way one day or another. But God is a God that will not leave me or forsake me. He is the God of second chance. He is the God that can heal me of all sickness, all unrighteousness. He can strengthen me. He can build me up where I am torn down. All he ask is that I put my trust in him, and have the faith to believe the impossible. In other words I need to have that crazy kind of faith that can move that mountain out of my way. Move my enemies out of my way. Move my family out of my way. Move my children, spouse out of my way. Because I am, determine to go all the way in Jesus name. My family can't stop me. My friends can't stop me. My enemy can't stop me. As long as I continue to walk blameless and upright in his word, I can have anything I ask in his name. I have the kind of faith that will move that mountain, and cause it to be still. Lord, I ask that you touch the circumstances in my life that may have altered my walk and has caused me to get off course. I ask Lord, that you take my spirits to another level in you. Take me higher and higher in you Lord. I want to be right. I want to be holy. I want to live my life so that others may see your glory and glorify you which is in heaven. Lord, I thank you and praise you for what you are doing, what you have already done in Jesus name I pray. Amen

"People who want to get rich fall into temptation and a trap and into many foolish and harmful desires that plunge men into ruin and destruction. For the love of money is a root of all kinds of evil. Some people, eager for money, have wandered from the faith and pierced themselves with many griefs." (I Timothy 6:9-10) NIV

"But if it's only money these leaders are after, they'll self-destruct in no time. Lust for money brings trouble and nothing but trouble. Going down that path, some lose their footing in the faith completely and live to regret it bitterly ever after." (I Timothy 6:9-10) Message Bible

Lord,

My God, we all have fallen short of this scripture in some way or another. I know that at times, I think about money and the lack of, and how I wish that I had more. Only to use it for my good, and not for the good of the kingdom of God. Then there are other times, I look and think about money to use it to help build up your kingdom. This has to be a great problem with all of us in this world today. We want more money, but are we willing to give more unto the kingdom or do we need it to buy a car, a house, furniture for the house, to entertain family and friends, to get things for our children. What is the motive behind having more money? I believe that it is a trick of the enemy, because the word of God says that he is our shepherd and we shall not be in want, we have everything that we need. He also told us in his word that he would meet all of our needs according to his riches in Christ Jesus. Then he said to us that through him we are more than conquerors. We are the lenders and not the borrower. He said if we delight ourselves in him he will give us the desires of our heart. Therefore, if we need a new car, or new house, or new furniture for that house, education, anything we need, all we have to do is delight ourselves in the word of God, and in him and he will give us the desires of our heart. Because we are his children, we have all that we need to make it. God, you ask me to trust you for whatever I need concerning my finances, and my needs. So Lord, I'm giving you all of my problems, whether they be financial, spiritually, mentally, physically, my marriage, my home, my children, my job, and my life I give over to you so that you can mold me and shape me to be who you want me to be. So that I can receive the blessings that you have in store for me. I thank you for blessing me, and keeping me on the cutting edge of your word. I know Lord that this walk is not an easy walk but if I press on to the higher call in Christ Jesus, I can make it. Because I can do all things through Christ Jesus who strengthen me. I give you the praise and the glory for truly you are worthy of it all. That is why I love you so much. I worship and adore you in the mighty name of Jesus I pray. Amen

"A time to search and a time to give up, a time to keep and a time to throw away, a time to tear and a time to mend, a time to be silent and a time to speak" (Ecclesiastes 3:6-7) NIV

"A right time to search and another to count your losses, A right time to hold on and another to let go, A right time to rip out and another to mend, A right time to shut up and another to speak up" (Ecclesiastes 3:6-7) Message Bible

God, Oh God,

What a powerful and life changing scripture this is. As a believer, we need to know that it is not necessary for us to always voice our opinion about things. Sometimes, God just want us to hear it and see and then go into our closet and pray about it. Many times, we are guilty of sharing what we have heard or seen with the he wrong person, and before you know it you are apart of a gossip that is spreading like wild fire. Instead of being a person who spreads the gossip, be the person who prays about it instead. That's what God would want. Even if you think it is not gossiping, but you think it is sharing information. In the eyes of the Lord, you are talking about something or someone that you should be praying about. If we would come together more and pray about things rather than talking about it, then just maybe the world and the people around us would be better. The next time you get ready to say something about someone please stop and think before you speak. Lord, help each of us to be slow to speak and quick to listen before we speak. Help us Lord, to apply the word of God to our mouth and to the words that we speak. Lord, I pray that we open up our eyes and ears to know that you really don't need our opinion, but you need more prayer from us. Prayer is the key that changes things and people. Lord, let me be and example to others, when they come up to me to talk, let me lead them in prayer instead of voicing my opinion about things. Lord, let the words of my mouth and the meditation of my heart be acceptable in thy sight daily. Lord, I thank you and I praise you for all that you have done in my life. I give you the glory and the praise in Jesus name I pray. Amen

"If his sons forsake my law and do not follow my statutes, if they violate my decrees and fail to keep my commands, I will punish their sin with the rod, their iniquity with flogging; but I will not take my love from him, nor will I ever betray my faithfulness. I will not violate my covenant or alter what my lips have uttered. Once for all, I have sworn by my holiness— and I will not lie to David-" (Psalm 89:30-35) NIV

"If his children refuse to do what I tell them, if they refuse to walk in the way I show them, If they spit on the directions I give them and tear up the rules I post for them— I'll rub their faces in the dirt of their rebellion and make them face the music. But I'll never throw them out, never abandon or disown them. Do you think I'd withdraw my holy promise? or take back words I'd already spoken? I've given my word, my whole and holy word; do you think I would lie to David?" (Psalm 89:30-35) Message Bible

Lord,

Reading this scripture reminds me of what you have told me to do. I didn't obey all the time, nor did I do what you told me to do. I'm thankful that you Lord did not give up on me nor did you let me go back to sinning. You did cause me to remember it over and over again in my spirit. You convicted me, and helped me to not to want to do it again. Because who you love you will discipline. I know that I made a promise to you when you saved, and delivered me from the world. I know that the words that I speak should be true. But, there goes that word again (but) when I made that promise to you, I didn't know that enemy would come at me and cause me not to be true to my word. I didn't know that I was going to have to suffer for it. Lord, I promised you if you would deliver me from lying, I would serve you until I die. Lord, I promised you that if you would get me out of jail, I would serve you until I die. I promised you if you would deliver me from fornication, I would serve you and live for you until I die. Lord, I promised you that if you would give me more money to help with my bills that I would become a better steward of my finances. Lord, I promised you that if you would deliver my children, that I would help someone else child to grow in your word. Lord, I promised you that if you would bless me with a job, I would work, and be on time, and do what I have to do to serve you at my job. Lord, I promised you that if you direct me to the right church, where I can grow spiritually, I would work for you each day and not give up on working for you. I promised you Lord, if you deliver me from alcoholism, I would turn my life over to you and work for you with my hands, helping to build up your kingdom. Lord, I promised you if you would deliver me from gossiping I would no longer speak ungodly things and talk about people. Lord, I promised you that if you would deliver me from the spirit of lust, I would keep my eyes on you and not on man. Lord, I promised you that I would serve you all the days of my life, no matter what it cost. Lord, I ask that you forgive me for making these promised and I did not fulfill it. I ask Lord, that you give me the strength to run this race. I ask Father, that you love me and help me to love other despite my pain and my words that I have said to others. Lord, I love you and I adore you for this awesome scripture that opens the eyes of every believer, and penetrates into every heart. It will give each of us a life changing experience if we apply this scripture to our life. Now, Lord, I give you all the glory and the honor in Jesus name I pray. Amen

"In my anguish I cried to the Lord, and he answered by setting me free. The Lord is with me; O will not be afraid, What can man do to me? The Lord is with me; he is my helper, I will look in triumph on my enemies, It is better to take refuge in the Lord than to trust in man. It is better to take refuge in the Lord than to trust in princes." (Psalm 118:5-8) NIV

"Pushed to the wall, I called to God; from the wide open spaces, he answered. God's now at my side and I'm not afraid; who would dare lay a hand on me? God's my strong champion; I flick off my enemies like flies. Far better to take refuge in God than trust in people; Far better to take refuge in God than trust in celebrities." (Psalm 118:5-8) Message Bible

My God,

    How many times have I felt like I was being pushed to the wall by family and friends? How often have I felt like they were using me or mistreating me. I trusted them in everything that they said and did. I trusted them to do what they told me they would do. I trusted them to help me when I needed help. I called upon the Lord, and he answered me. he delivered me from my enemies. He delivered me from myself. God was with me when my family and friends mistreated me or they used me. But I thank my God for teaching my how to put my trust in him and not in my family not in my friends, not in my co-workers, not in my spouse, not in my pastor, not in my circumstances, only in HIM. I thank you Lord, for speaking to my heart, and creating in me a right spirit. I thank you Lord, for lifting me up and turning me around and placing my feet on solid ground. I thank you that when I am in trouble, I can come to you, and you will deliver me. That's why I can give you the praise and the glory, because I look to the hills from whence cometh my help. You are my light in dark places. You are my strength. You are my protector. You are my provider. I love you and I adore you. In Jesus name, I pray. Amen

"When I shut up the heavens so that there is no rain, or command locusts to devour the land or send a plague among my people, if my people, who are called by my name, will humble themselves and pray and seek my face and turn from their wicked ways, then will I hear from heaven and will forgive their sin and will heal their land. Now my eyes will be open and my ears attentive to the prayers offered in this place. I have chosen and consecrated this temple so that my Name may be there forever. My eyes and my heart will always be there." (2 Chronicles 7: 13-16) NIV

"If I ever shut off the supply of rain from the skies or order the locusts to eat the crops or send a plague on my people, and my people, my God-defined people, respond by humbling themselves, praying, seeking my presence, and turning their backs on their wicked lives, I'll be there ready for you: I'll listen from heaven, forgive their sins, and restore their land to health. From now on I'm alert day and night to the prayers offered at this place. Believe me, I've chosen and sanctified this Temple that you have built: My Name is stamped on it forever; my eyes are on it and my heart in it always." (2 Chronicles 7:13-16) Message Bible

Oh Lord,

How great is thy name in all the earth. You are wonderful, awesome, glorious, and powerful. I thank you Lord for your word and your promises. Lord, I have to ask you where are the people who are called by your name, and why haven't they been praying, and if they are praying what are they praying for. Because when I look around I see what is going on in this world. I know that your word has to be fulfilled. But I also, know that your word says if your people who are called by your name would humble themselves and pray. So tell me Lord, where are the true prayer warriors, and true Christians. Are they sitting in judgment, or they wanting on someone else to pray for them? Lord, I want to know where and what is going on with your people today. If we were truly praying, then the children would be safe, not harmed by sex offenders. If we were truly praying then men and women would not be killing each other. If we were really praying our churches would not be in the shape they are in. If we were really praying, people would not be unemployed, but would own their own. If we were praying and seeking your face, then our nation would not be in such a mess. Lord, help us to pray. Teach us to pray for and intercede for each other, for the nation, and for our families. Because you told us in your word, that where one or two are gathered in your name touching and agreeing there you will be also. Why aren't we touching and agreeing on the things of this world? Lord, I have questions, and I need answers to. Why Lord is there so much torment? Why? Because we are not taking you at your word, alot of us read the word and don't apply the word to our life nor to our prayer life. The word is what going to get us to the next level in God. So, today, Lord, I lift up my voice to you and I pray that all of your people would come together, seek your face, turn from there wicked ways, humble themselves, and pray in Jesus name. I thank you Lord, for your promise to heal this land if we pray, and seek you. I thank you Lord, for listening to our prayers. I thank you for giving each of us the words to pray. I thank you for your love, and your power that worked in us. In the name of Jesus I pray. Amen

"You, dear children, are from God and have overcome them, because the one who is in you is greater than the one who is in the world. They are from the world and therefore speak from the viewpoint of the world, and the world listens to them. We are from God, and whoever knows God listens to us; but whoever is not from God does not listen to us. This is how we recognize the Spirit of truth and the spirit of falsehood." (1 John 4:4-6) NIV

"My dear children, you come from God and belong to God. You have already won a big victory over those false teachers, for the Spirit in you is far stronger than anything in the world. These people belong to the Christ-denying world. They talk the world's language and the world eats it up. But we come from God and belong to God. Anyone who knows God understands us and listens. The person who has nothing to do with God will, of course, not listen to us. This is another test for telling the Spirit of Truth from the spirit of deception." (1 John 4:-6) Message Bible

My God,

    Thank you Jesus. When the world seems to close in on me I don't have to worry because I belong to God. When it seems like my life is at its end, I don't have to worry because I belong to God. When people talk about me, and call me out of my name, I don't have to worry because God's got my back. When I feel like giving up, I don't because God will give me the strength to run this race. When the world is against me, I know that God is for me and he is more than the world against me. When I fall down, I know that my God will be there to pick me up. When people lie on me, I know that God will fight my battle for me. When I'm down and out, I know that God will lift my spirit up. God is a good God, and what he has said will come to pass if I have faith to believe and to receive. Lord, I thank you for what you are doing in my life. I thank you for what you are doing through me. I thank you that you have given me wisdom, knowledge and understanding of your word. Lord, I ask that you manifest your power over my life right now. I ask dear Lord that your will be done in my life. I give you the praise and the glory in Jesus name I pray. Amen

"Are we beginning to commend ourselves again? Or do we need, like some people, letters of recommendation to you or from you? You yourselves are our letter, written on our hearts, known and read by everybody. You show that you are a letter from Christ, the result of our ministry, written not with ink but with the Spirit of the living God, not on tablets of stone but on tablets of human hearts." (2 Corinthians 3:1-3) NIV

"Does it sound like we're patting ourselves on the back, insisting on our credentials, asserting our authority? Well, we're not. Neither do we need letters of endorsement, either to you or from you. You yourselves are all the endorsement we need. Your very lives are a letter that anyone can read by just looking at you. Christ himself wrote it—not with ink, but with God's living Spirit; not chiseled into stone, but carved into human lives—and we publish it." (2 Corinthians 3:1-3) Message Bible

My God,

    The bible lets me know that Jesus is my example and He came to show me how to live. How I handle myself in front of other people shows them how they should live. According to this scripture, we are to be living epistles read of all men - lights shining out brightly in a dark world. There are some people who do not attend church, nor do they read their bibles, so we as Saints of God are there only bible that they read, and the only light that will reflect Christ in their life. As a saint of God I have to be very careful of how I treat the people that I met, because I never know if they are believers or not. The only way that I would know is in our conversation. So, Lord, I ask that my walk will be season with salt, and that my light will shine before men and women everywhere so that they may glorify You which is in heaven. Lord, don't allow me to cause any of your children the saved and the unsaved to stumble and fall by the wayside. I know Lord that I am to treat everyone with love and kindness, regardless of what I may think they have done or what others may want be to believer about them. I have to allow my emotions and my feelings to die, so that I can lift my brother and sister up in Christ Jesus. I have to ask myself what would Jesus do in this matter, not what I have done or what I think I should do, or what my flesh seems to be thinking about them. Because we are all God's children's, no matter what. Because after all it's not about me, my emotions, my thoughts, nor my plans, it is all about God. Lord, if I have cause someone to stop coming to church to hear your word, because of what I may have said to them, or the way I may have treated them wrongly, please forgive me. Help me to go back and make mends with them Lord. Because I don't every want to be the cause of them not growing spiritually. Let me truly live my life according to what your word says and not what my emotions and what others may tell me. Because it is for you I live and for you I die. Therefore, Lord, I surrender and I ask for forgiveness right now if I have done any of these things to any one of your children. Lord, I thank you for forgiving me, and causing me to forgive and forget what I done in Jesus name I pray. I give you the glory and the honor in Jesus name I pray. Amen

"Therefore, since we have a great high priest who has gone through the heavens, Jesus the Son of God, let us hold firmly to the faith we profess. For we do not have a high priest who is unable to sympathize with our weaknesses, but we have one who has been tempted in every way, just as we are—yet was without sin. Let us then approach the throne of grace with confidence, so that we may receive mercy and find grace to help us in our time of need." (Hebrews 4:14-16) NIV

"Now that we know what we have—Jesus, this great High Priest with ready access to God—let's not let it slip through our fingers. We don't have a priest who is out of touch with our reality. He's been through weakness and testing, experienced it all—all but the sin. So let's walk right up to him and get what he is so ready to give. Take the mercy, accept the help." (Hebrews 4:14-16) Message Bible

My God,

Thank you Jesus for being the great High priest who has ready access to God. You went through alot for me. You did all of that for me, but yet sometimes I am not willing to do anything for you. You were without sin in all that you did, but I allow the enemy to sometimes come in and get me off course and yes, I sin. I sin when I talk about others. I sin when I pass judgment on others. Lord, I sin when I think things that are not pure, trustworthy, or of a good repore. Lord, it is easy to fall into sin, in this day and time, but as a believer I should know that it is all a trick of the enemy. Because if I stay focus on the word of God and study and to show myself approve by you, then I shall overcome temptation. Lord, I pray that you would guide me in all areas of my life, and guard my mouth and my lips, let nothing come out of my mouth that is not to lift your people up or to encourage someone. Touch me Lord with your power and your might that my walk may be straight in all that I do. Make every crocked edge straight in my life. Bless my going and my coming in Jesus name I pray. Amen.

"This is how we know what love is: Jesus Christ laid down his life for us. And we ought to lay down our lives for our brothers. If anyone has material possessions and sees his brother in need but has no pity on him, how can the love of God be in him? Dear children, let us not love with words or tongue but with actions and in truth. This then is how we know that we belong to the truth, and how we set our hearts at rest in his presence whenever our hearts condemn us. For God is greater than our hearts, and he knows everything." (I John 3:16-20) NIV

"This is how we've come to understand and experience love: Christ sacrificed his life for us. This is why we ought to live sacrificially for our fellow believers, and not just be out for ourselves. If you see some brother or sister in need and have the means to do something about it but turn a cold shoulder and do nothing, what happens to God's love? It disappears. And you made it disappear. My dear children, let's not just talk about love; let's practice real love. This is the only way we'll know we're living truly, living in God's reality. It's also the way to shut down debilitating self-criticism, even when there is something to it. For God is greater than our worried hearts and knows more about us than we do ourselves." (I John 3:16-20) Message Bible

My Lord,

Contrary to some opinions, being a Christian has nothing to do with where we were born, or with where we spent Sunday mornings every week during our childhood. We aren't a Christian because we go to church... just like we're not a hamburger because you go to McDonald's. You become a Christian when you practice the principles that are set before in the Word of God. God's word is true, and it is our instruction for everyday living. God laid down his life for us, why O why can't we laid down our life for someone else. If we see one of our brothers or sister in need the bible tells us that we are to met their needs. After all this body, that home, that car, and that job does not belong to us anyway. everything belongs to God. So if he asked us to do something to help a brother or sister out, then why come we can't or want do it? In essence we are being disobedient to the word of God. We shouldn't have to wait on someone to tell us to bless someone else, if you know of the need, whether it be financial, mentally or physically then we should met that need. I'm reminded of a good friend who needed a transplant and God spoke to me and told me to be the donor, why, because this isn't my body it belongs to God. So, I went to that person and told her and she rejoices and cried for along time. Only one of her family members stepped up and gave her the transparent. But I wanted her to know I was willing and obedient to what God had told me to do. Many of you reading this right now may think I was crazy, but I'm not I just obey the voice of the Lord. When God speaks something to you don't just sit on it do it right then. Your reward will come from God for being obedient to his word. Lord, I thank you that I heard your voice and obey. I thank you that you will use me to meet the need of one of my brothers or sisters. I thank you for your love and your power. I thank you Lord, for your protection. I give you the glory and the honor in Jesus name I pray. Amen

"Jude, a servant of Jesus Christ and a brother of James. To those who have been called, who are loved by God the Father and kept by Jesus Christ: Mercy, peace and love be yours in abundance." (Jude 1-2) NIV

"I, Jude, am a slave to Jesus Christ and brother to James, writing to those loved by God the Father, called and kept safe by Jesus Christ. Relax, everything's going to be all right; rest, everything's coming together; open your hearts, love is on the way! "(Jude 1-2) Message Bible

Oh my God,

Thank you for loving me even when I've gone my own way. Thank you for protecting me, even when I pushed you away. Thank you for your mercy, and your grace, that I really don't deserve, but you bless me with it each and everyday. Thank you for your peace that surpasses all my understanding. Lord, I know that I get discouraged at times, because I don't understand what is going on in my life. But I have joy knowing that your word tells me to relax, because everything will be all right. Rest, because everything's coming together. Open up my heart and love is on the way. I can relax knowing that my children will be saved, delivered, and set free from all bondages in Jesus Christ name. I can relax because I know that all my bills will be paid, and I will be debt free. I can relax knowing that troubles don't last always. I can relax knowing that money cometh to me right now in the name of Jesus. I can rest in the safety of Your arms. I can rest in knowing that all of my worrying days are behind me, and I can look forward to what lies ahead. Lord, have I stopped today to tell you how much I love you and adore you? Well I do, in more ways than one. I give you all the glory and the praise for what you are doing in my life, even though I can't see the outcome right now. I will still lift you up and extol your name. I don't have to wait until I see my victory or my blessing I can praise you while I'm in my storm or situation. Praise is the best result when I am going through a storm in my life. Lord, I lift your name on high. I extol you O Lord, because you are wonderful. You are awesome. You do miracles. You are my all and all. I love you and I give you my all and all in Jesus name I pray. Amen

"And so we know and rely on the love God has for us. God is love. Whoever lives in love lives in God, and God in him. In this way, love is made complete among us so that we will have confidence on the day of judgment, because in this world we are like him. There is no fear in love. But perfect love drives out fear, because fear has to do with punishment. The one who fears is not made perfect in love." (I John 4:16-18) NIV

"We know it so well, we've embraced it heart and soul, this love that comes from God. God is love. When we take up permanent residence in a life of love, we live in God and God lives in us. This way, love has the run of the house, becomes at home and mature in us, so that we're free of worry on Judgment Day—our standing in the world is identical with Christ's. There is no room in love for fear. Well-formed love banishes fear. Since fear is crippling, a fearful life—fear of death, fear of judgment—is one not yet fully formed in love." (I John 4:16-18) Message Bible

My God,

   Thank you for loving me. Teaching me how to live in love and to live in God. I know that I am to have confident that on that Day of Judgment, my love will be complete, because in the world I am suppose to be like You. I have no fear, because love drives out fear, and love has no punishment, therefore, I shall not fear. Lord, if God is love and I am to live like Him, then why is it so hard for me to show love to my brother and sisters in this world. Why is it Lord that we seem to tear down our brothers and sisters instead of showing them the God kind of Love. Why do we backbite, stab them in their backs, and judge them on there past? The reason why is because the God kind of love is not really in us, we say it is but is it? Because if it truly were, then we would not have a problem showing that kind of love to one another. Even in our homes, in our churches, on our jobs, and everywhere we go. We need to take an assessment of how we are treating others. Because the Bible tells us to "Do unto others as we would have them do unto us." If you don't want anyone to mistreat you, then why do you mistreat your brother and sisters. Lord, I pray and ask that you forgive me if I have mistreated any of my brothers and sisters by my word, my actions, and my deeds. Let the God kind of love abide within me, and through me this day and forever more. Lord, I thank you and I praise you for your love, your power, and your anointing that rest, rules, and abides within me this day. In Jesus name I pray. Amen

"Love the LORD, all his saints! The LORD preserves the faithful, but the proud he pays back in full. Be strong and take heart, all you who hope in the LORD." (Psalm 31:23-24) NIV

"Love God, all you saints; God takes care of all who stay close to him, But he pays back in full those arrogant enough to go it alone. Be brave. Be strong. Don't give up. Expect God to get here soon." (Psalm 31:23-24) Message Bible

Dear Lord,

I don't every want to be proud that I can't be committed to following you or loving you. I don't every want you to give up on me. I know that your love is unconditional, and that's the type of love that I should have for you and your children. I try very hard Lord, to be in your will, and to do your will and to follow your commandments. each time that I try to do my best something keeps telling me that you are not there and that I will fail if I do it God's way. That's the reason why I always seem to get in trouble for doing it my way and not trusting you enough to do it. I know you love me, you have said it over and over again in your word. But when I'm going through those storms it seems like I am all along, and there is no one for me to talk to. No one for me to lay my head on their shoulder and cry. No one to hold me while I'm crying. It feels like I'm in this world all by myself. Lord, tell me where you are then. I know you said you will never leave me, nor forsake me, but it is at those times in my life that I need you the most, but I don't feel you near me. Lord, I know you know my pain, and my sorrow; you even know how many hairs are in my head. You know my hearts desire. But I need to know that you are there for me. Yes, I read my Bible. Yes, I go to church. But it's when I'm not in church and I'm not in the presence of my bible that the enemy will come against me, what do I do then Lord. I hear you speaking to me now Lord, You told me that it is then that I should call upon the name of Jesus, and boldly proclaim your word and your power over my life. Lord, I won't give in and I won't give up. I will continue to press toward the high calling in Christ Jesus. Because I know that my savior lives in me. I know I will be tempted, and the trials will come, and the weapons will form. But I also know Lord that they will not, and shall not prosper in any way shape form or fashion. Because I am a child of the most high King. My Father which art in heaven watches over me and he shall cover me daily with his blood. He will see me through all of this and much, much, more. I love Him, and He loves me. I give you the praise and the glory in Jesus name I pray. Amen

"Here I am! I stand at the door and knock. If anyone hears my voice and opens the door, I will come in and eat with him, and he with me. To him who overcomes, I will give the right to sit with me on my throne, just as I overcame and sat down with my Father on his throne." (Revelation 3:20-21) NIV

"Look at me. I stand at the door. I knock. If you hear me call and open the door, I'll come right in and sit down to supper with you. Conquerors will sit alongside me at the head table, just as I, having conquered, took the place of honor at the side of my Father. That's my gift to the conquerors!" (Revelation 3:20-21) Message Bible

My God,

You are awesome. You are truly worthy of the honor and the glory. I bow down before you and I worship your holy name. Oh Lord, open up the door to my heart so that you can come in and eat with me. Many of us today are in the church but yet, you are not living in our heart. Because if you were living in our hearts we would not be gossipers. We would not voice our opinion about the things that others do or say. You didn't put us here for that you told us to judge not that ye be judge. When we voice our opinion about something that is being judgmental, because you don't need our opinion you simply need us to pray more. As believers we have to stop and really read the word and apply it to our everyday life. We are the real reason that our churches are not full. Because we talk too much about the foolish things of this world, and we are not praying enough for the word of God to go forth in our life, and in the life of others. This scripture means alot to all of us today, because in order to do God's will, and to be in His will we have to allow him to come into our heart and change us from the inside out. Change our way of thinking. Change our way of talking. Change our way of walking. Yes, change our hearts toward our brothers and sisters. Many of us say we love the Lord, but yet don't love our biological sister/ brother let along our Christian brother/sister. Come on now, that is not of God. We have to love on each other with the kind of Love that God would have. After all he loved us enough to give up his Son for each of us. If we say that the Lord is in our heart, but yet can't speak to one another then we are lying and the truth is not in us. If we say we have God in our heart and still hold a grudge against someone, then we are lying and the truth is not in us. The bible tells us to love our enemy and pray for them. Lord, help each of us today to truly search our heart and our mind, if you find anything that is not pleasing in your sight, anything at all please Lord remove it right now in the mighty name of Jesus. Help us Father to not hold grudges against anyone we say we love. You told us to forgive seventy times seventy, help us to do so in the name of Jesus. Let the words of our mouth and the meditation of our heart be acceptable in thy sight O Lord, our Redeemer. Lord, I feel you knocking at the door of my heart, and I will open up my heart and allow you entrance. Lord, I will allow your word to come into my heart and apply it to my life so that I may not sin against you. Lord, I thank you for this word and for this divine revelation of your word in Jesus name I pray. Amen

"Be joyful always; pray continually; give thanks in all circumstances, for this is God's will for you in Christ Jesus." (I Thessalonians 5:16-18) NIV

"Be cheerful no matter what; pray all the time; thank God no matter what happens. This is the way God wants you who belong to Christ Jesus to live." (I Thessalonians 5:16-18) Message Bible

My God,

      I heard you, and I will obey. I will rejoice when my bills are due and I don't know where the money is coming from. I will rejoice and be glad when my children are being wayward and disobedient. I will pray continually and give thanks in all circumstances and situations in my life. I will thank you God for my spouse who never does anything around the house, nor help with the children. I will thank you when the enemy comes and put sickness in my body, because I know that You have paid the ultimate price for me to be healed. Thank you Lord for saving my family, my friends, my co-workers, and everyone that I know from themselves and from the enemy. Lord, help each us not to complain and remain in the situations that we are in. But help us Lord, to praise you and be raised up out of it all. I remember a phrase that Joyce Meyers said, **"We can complain and remain, or praise and be raised."** When I read this it brought joy to my spirit to know that no matter how much the enemy will try to bring me down in my finances, with my children, with my spouse, and on my job, I can still praise God for raising me out of it all. Because God is my Revealer and my Mediator of all that will be done in my life. That's why I give Him praise and glory for all that He does for me, through me, and to me. My God is an awesome God. Lord, I will not complain. I will not remain. I will praise and I will be raised in Jesus name. Amen

"For God so loved the world that he gave his one and only Son, that whoever believes in him shall not perish but have eternal life. For God did not send his Son into the world to condemn the world, but to save the world through him. Whoever believes in him is not condemned, but whoever does not believe stands condemned already because he has not believed in the name of God's one and only Son." (John 3:16-18) NIV

"This is how much God loved the world: He gave his Son, his one and only Son. And this is why: so that no one need be destroyed; by believing in him, anyone can have a whole and lasting life. God didn't go to all the trouble of sending his Son merely to point an accusing finger, telling the world how bad it was. He came to help, to put the world right again. Anyone who trusts in him is acquitted; anyone who refuses to trust him has long since been under the death sentence without knowing it. And why? Because of that person's failure to believe in the one-of-a-kind Son of God when introduced to him." (John 3:16-18) Message Bible

Father,

I am so sorry that I have not taken your word to heart. This is an awesome word from God to me. Because if God was willing to give up his only son for me, why can't I give up my sins for him. You see Lord, I am guilty of lying to others, talking about others, alerting the truth to fit me. I am guilty Lord of not being a good steward of your money you have giving me through my job. I am guilty Lord, of not spending my time in your word like I should. It seems like every thing has come before you. I am guilty Lord of not attending my church like I need to. I'm guilty Lord, for sleeping around and I'm not even married. I'm guilty of lusting after someone who is not my spouse. I'm guilty Lord, of gambling, cheating, and holding back my tithes for my pleasure. I'm guilty Lord of letting my feelings and emotions get in the way of you blessing me. I'm guilty and I repent of all of these sins right now in the mighty name of Jesus. But, Lord, if you were willing to give up Your Son for me, then why can't I give up these many sins for you to live in my life and through me. Help me Father, to be obedient; I know that this is a sacrifice to give up all of those sins for you so that I can have a relationship with you. Lord, disciple me, so that I can get this right. You told me that you are my shepherd and I shall not be in want. You told me Lord, that you will never leave me nor forsake me. You told me Lord, that you would order my footsteps, and direct my pathway. You told me all of this and much, much more, but yet, I still have not totally surrendered my all and all to you. Lord, I know you love me because if you didn't you would not have given up your only Son for me. I know you care, because if you didn't you would not listen to what I'm saying this morning. I know you hear my prayer and my cry this morning; I ask that you move upon it in your Son name. Oh Lord, I need you to touch my heart, my mind and my spirit, and anything that is keeping me from you I ask right now that you remove in the name of Jesus. Lord, I thank you and I praise you for renewing my mind, renewing my soul, renewing my spirit. I thank you for giving me another chance to get this right with you. I thank you for loving me enough to give up your Son for me. Thank you for your grace and your mercy in Jesus name I pray. Amen.

"Is any one of you in trouble? He should pray. Is anyone happy? Let him sing songs of praise. Is any one of you sick? He should call the elders of the church to pray over him and anoint him with oil in the name of the Lord. And the prayer offered in faith will make the sick person well; the Lord will raise him up. If he has sinned, he will be forgiven." (James 5:13-15) NIV

"Are you hurting? Pray. Do you feel great? Sing. Are you sick? Call the church leaders together to pray and anoint you with oil in the name of the Master. Believing-prayer will heal you, and Jesus will put you on your feet. And if you've sinned, you'll be forgiven—healed inside and out." (James 5:13-15) Message Bible

Heavenly Father,

      I attend to Your Word. I incline my ears to your sayings. I will not let them depart from my eyes. I keep them in the midst of my heart, for they are life and healing to all my flesh. Proverbs 4:20-22. As you were with Moses, so are you with me. My eyes are not dim; neither is my natural vigor diminished. Blessed are my eyes for they see and my ears for they hear. Deuteronomy 34:7. "No evil will befall me; neither shall any plague come near my dwelling. For you have given angels charge over me. They keep me in all ways." In my pathway is life, healing, and health. Psalms 91:10-11; Proverbs 12:28. "Jesus took my infirmities and bore my sicknesses. Therefore I refuse to allow sickness to dominate my body. The life of God flows within me, bringing healing to every fiber of my being. Matthew 8:16; John 6:63. I am redeemed from the curse. Galatians 3:13 is flowing in my Blood stream. It flows to every cell of my body restoring life and health. Mark 11:23-24; Luke 17:6. The life of 1 Peter 2:24 is a reality in my flesh, restoring every cell of my body. My body is the temple of the Holy Ghost. I make a demand on my body to release the right chemicals and hormones. My body is in perfect chemical balance. My pancreas secretes the proper amount of insulin for life and health. Mark 11:23-24. Now Lord, according to your word in I Peter 2:24 states, I have been healed by the stripes of Jesus. Cancer, sugar diabetes, heart disease, obesity, high blood pressure, sickle cell, leukemia, pneumonia, back pain, headaches, AIDS, Thyroid, sinuses, flu, bad eye sight, poor hearing, ear problems, tumors, cyst, afflictions, infections or any other disease can not enter my body in the name of Jesus. Lord, I thank you for healing and strengthen my body. I thank you that no weapon formed against my body shall prosper. I thank you Lord for your word and your promise for me to be in good health as my soul prospers. I give you he glory and the honor in the mighty name of Jesus I pray. Amen

"My mouth will speak words of wisdom; the utterance from my heart will give understanding. I will turn my ear to a proverb; with the harp I will expound my riddle" (Psalm 49:3-4) NIV

"I set plainspoken wisdom before you, my heart-seasoned understandings of life. I fine-tuned my ear to the sayings of the wise, I solve life's riddle with the help of a harp." (Psalm 49:3-4) Message Bible

Oh Lord my God and my Father,

Thank you for giving me words to speak over my life. Words that will encourage me in all my doing. Words that I can speak over my family, over my spouse, over, my finances, over my children, over my job, over my church family, and over me. Lord, you spoke a word over each of us and we were birthed into a new life with you. Lord, I speak prosperity over my finances. Lord, I speak healing to my body and my family body as well. Lord, I speak joy into every dead situation in my life. I speak peace into every worry bones in my bone. I speak increase in my life. Increase in my finances, increase in wisdom, increase in knowledge of your word. I speak to every dry bone in my bone and in my family and friends life, I tell those dry bones to line up with the word of God and straight out and walk right in the name of Jesus. I speak over my marriage that what God has joined together that no man, woman, finances, or any situation shall tear us apart. We will love each other in sickness, in the good the bad times, and in riches and in poor times in the mighty name of Jesus. I speak a word over my children that they shall be great doctors, lawyer, prophet, and missionaries, teachers of the Word of God, and mighty men and women of God. I declare them to be saved sanctified, and full of the Holy Ghost right now in the name of Jesus. No weapon formed against my children, or my grandchildren shall prosper and every tongue that rises up in judgment against them shall be condemned in the name of Jesus. They are the head and not the tail. they are above and not beneath. They are blessed coming in, and going out in the name of Jesus. We are blessed because we are a seed of Abraham and because we are a seed we have everything that we need in the name of Jesus. Father, I cancel every scheme every attack of the enemy right now against my family and my life in the name of Jesus. I plead the blood of Jesus over their life and my life as well. We are more than conquerors. We can do all things through Christ Jesus who strengthens us. We are debt free and walking in prosperity in the name of Jesus. Thank you Lord for your word that it can and will be manifested in all of our life, because we have faith to believe and it shall come to past. In Jesus name I pray. Amen

"I will look on you with favor and make you fruitful and increase your numbers, and I will keep my covenant with you. You will still be eating last year's harvest when you will have to move it out to make room for the new." (Leviticus 26:9-10) NIV

"I'll give you my full attention: I'll make sure you prosper, make sure you grow in numbers, and keep my covenant with you in good working order. You'll still be eating from last year's harvest when you have to clean out the barns to make room for the new crops." (Leviticus 26:9-10) Message Bible

My God,

    What an awesome revelation to know that you will favor us and make us fruitful and increase our numbers, as long as we come in agreement with your covenant. The only way that we can agree with this covenant is to submit unto your will and your word. I don't have to worry about what I shall eat, because you have already assured me that I shall eat from last year's harvest. I need to stop and think more about what I need to be sowing into so I can reap a harvest from it. So what every I sowed (planted) last year I shall reap now. If I sowed good seeds on good grounds, than I shall reap that harvest. If I sowed a bad seed (giving grudgingly) than I shall reap grudgingly. If I sowed love than I shall reap a harvest of love. If I sowed gossip than I shall reap gossip. If I sowed an attitude than I shall reap an attitude. If I sowed patience, than I shall reap patience. If I sowed in my prayer life, than I shall reap a harvest from my prayers. If I sowed my time into the ministry, than I shall reap more time for the ministry. God has assured me that whatever I sowed into I shall get an increase in it. Lord, forgive me if I have every sowed a seed into the wrong ground. If I have sinned please forgive me of any and all sins, omission, and commission. Lord, I thank you and I praise you for your word and your promises for my life. I thank you because you are truly worthy of the praise and the glory. You along are worthy of the praise and the glory. I extol you. I bow down and worship before you. Lord, I love you and I appreciate all that you do and all that you are about to do in my life and through my life in Jesus name. Amen

"And may these words of mine, which I have prayed before the LORD, be near to the LORD our God day and night, that he may uphold the cause of his servant and the cause of his people Israel according to each day's need, so that all the peoples of the earth may know that the LORD is God and that there is no other. But your hearts must be fully committed to the LORD our God, to live by his decrees and obey his commands, as at this time." (I Kings 8:59-61) NIV

"And let these words that I've prayed in the presence of God be always right there before him, day and night, so that he'll do what is right for me, to guarantee justice for his people Israel day after day after day. Then all the people on earth will know God is the true God; there is no other God. And *you*, your lives must be totally obedient to God, our personal God, following the life path he has cleared, alert and attentive to everything he has made plain this day." (I Kings 8: 59 - 61) Message Bible

My God,

When you call me to do something for your Kingdom, I have to be committed to my call. I can't do it today and then forget about it until I want to do it again. That is not how it works. My heart must be fully committed to the Lord my God, I have to live by his decrees and obey his commands. I must be fully committed to my life of prayer. I must be fully committed to my church. I must be fully committed to my work for the ministries that God has ordained me for. I must be fully committed to my pastor, because he is my spiritual father, and my leader. I must be fully willing to obey all the bylaws, and rules of my church. I must be committed to attending Bible Study, Sunday School, Sunday services, and any and all other ministries events. As a child of God, I have to be committed in order that I may be available to help someone else along the way. Many of times we get so busy with our everyday activities that we forget that God is first in our live. Yes, I know you have to work, but don't forget it was God who blessed you with that job in the first place. Why not give him some of your time for his kingdom building. Yes, I know that we all have children and they are in activities at school, but it was God who gave you that child, and he told us to train them up in the way they should go. Shouldn't we train them to be in attendance at church so that the word can be deposit in their life. Yes, I know you are working on your degree, but wasn't it God who gave you the wisdom, and the knowledge to continue on in your education. Yes, I know you are married, and your husband doesn't go to church, but wasn't it God who saved, and delivered you and gave you the opportunity to sanctify your spouse by letting your light shine before them. After all God was so committed to each of us that he gave up his Son for us. My God I thank you for teaching me how to commit my ways, my times, and my actions unto you. I thank you Lord, for teaching me how to commit even in situations that are out of my hand. Lord, I don't take it for granted the things that you have done for me and what you are about to do through me. I don't take it for granted how you blessed me, and kept me. Lord, I can't thank you enough for your love, and your grace, and your mercy. I give you all the praise and the glory in Christ Jesus name I pray. Amen

"Do not cast me from your presence or take your Holy Spirit from me. Restore to me the joy of your salvation and grant me a willing spirit, to sustain me." (Psalm 51:11-12) NIV

"Don't throw me out with the trash, or fail to breathe holiness in me. Bring me back from gray exile; put a fresh wind in my sails!" (Psalm 51:11-12) Message Bible

Oh Lord,

    Help me Lord to get my zeal back for the ministry and the church. You see Lord, I have been wounded, and I have been hurt by what others have done to me. I do not feel like getting up on Sunday morning and going to church to look them in their face only to be reminded of what they said about me. I do not even want to work in the ministry that I am supposed to be in. I have been hurt so bad, Lord. I know you know Lord, but I need someone I can talk to. Someone who understands my pain and my situation. I need you to lead me and show me what it is I am supposed to do about all of this Lord. Lord, I'm tired of the every day activities, I go to work, and then I go to do ministry work. But I don't have a zeal for it anymore Lord. Why oh why Lord do the very people who say they are Christian seem to be the very one who hurt others in the church? Can you tell me why Lord. Where is my joy for the ministry Lord, what happen to it? Many of us today have felt like this in many ways. But God said that he will never leave you nor forsake you. He is always right with you. I know that the joy that I have, the world didn't give it to me and the world can't take it away. I come this far by faith, trusting and believing in his holy name. I can't turn around. God has been too good for me to quit now. He is doing a great work in me, and through me. All I have to do is surrender my will to His will. I can't worry about people, what they say or do. Because life is too short. God has been there for me when I was sick, he healed me. When I needed strength he gave it to me. What ever I needed I founded it in His word, and not in the word of people. I don't go to church because of people, and not to fit in, but I go to hear a word from the Lord that will help me to grow stronger in his word. I can't be worry or bother by what other may think about me, or say about me. All I can say to them is I'm glad you saw fit to speak about me, because that puts me in the number with Jesus, they talk about him everyday. I'm glad to be in that number. Lord, I ask right now that you lift the spirit of heaviness and despair from me right now in the name of Jesus. Open my eyes Lord that I only see what you would have me to see. Open my ears that I only hear what you will have me to hear. Touch me Lord, and give me every ounce of my zeal and joy back that I have allowed the enemy to take from me right now in the name of Jesus. Cover me with your blood Lord, so that I will not sin against you in anyway, shape, or fashion. Keep my eyes focus on you and you only Lord. Let my light shine so that others may see your good works and glorify you, which is in heaven. Let me tell someone today of your goodness and mercy. Thank you Lord, for your word, and your promises for my life. Help me to apply these principles to my life. I give you the glory and the honor. In Jesus name, I pray. Amen

"Jesus used this figure of speech, but they did not understand what he was telling them. Therefore, Jesus said again, "I tell you the truth, I am the gate for the sheep. All who ever came before me were thieves and robbers, but the sheep did not listen to them. I am the gate; whoever enters through me will be saved. He will come in and go out, and find pasture. The thief comes only to steal and kill and destroy; I have come that they may have life, and have it to the full." (John 10:6-10) NIV

"Jesus told this simple story, but they had no idea what he was talking about. So he tried again. "I'll be explicit, then. I am the Gate for the sheep. All those others are up to no good—sheep stealers, every one of them. But the sheep didn't listen to them. I am the Gate. Anyone who goes through me will be cared for—will freely go in and out, and find pasture. A thief is only there to steal, kill, and destroy. I came so they can have real and eternal life, more and better life than they ever dreamed of." (John 10:6-10) Message

My God,

  Thank you for this word to encourage me in my walk. Lord, I do not know why at times I allow the enemy to come into my life and try to steal my joy, my peace, and even my family from me. I know your word told me that he will come to steal kill and destroy, and you came that I may have life. Many times when I'm going through my uphill and my pain, I don't apply your word to my life like I should, so I allow the enemy to come in. He has come in and stole my finances from me, causing me to be in more debt than I care to be in. He has stolen my children from me; they do not want to be around me because I try to tell them what is right and wrong according to the word. He has come in and started confusion in my home between my spouse and myself. Only because I did not speak the word over it. I allowed him to come in because of the words of my mouth. Instead of me, speaking life into every dead situation allowed the devil to speak through me and now he has taken control. Lord, forgive me for allowing the enemy to take my word from me. But today Lord, I come to serve him notice, that the words that I speak are words of wisdom, knowledge and understanding of your written word. I come to apply those words to what the enemy has tried to take from me. I come to take back everything that the locust and the enemy have tried to steal from my family and me I speak healing over my body. I speak total restoration over my health and my body. I speak prosperity over my finances. I speak more than enough over my finances. I speak money cometh to me right now in the mighty name of Jesus. I speak good measures pressed down, shaken together, running over on my finances. I speak debt cancellation in the name of Jesus. I was down but now I'm the head and not the tail. I have more than enough. Because my Daddy shall supply all my needs according to his riches in Christ Jesus. I speak debt free over every bill in my household in this 2009 in the name of Jesus. I speak to my children's life and mind, they shall be great men and women of God, and they shall walk in the anointing and calling that God has over and on their life. I speak to every prophetic word that has been spoken over their life to be manifested right now in the mighty name of Jesus. Manifested it today Jesus. I speak prosperity over there life. I speak wisdom and knowledge of God's word over their life. I speak to my marriage and I call it healed, walking side by side in the name of Jesus. I speak to my spouse, you shall be a great man or woman of God you shall exceed in every level of blessings that God has for your life. You shall walk in that prophetic anointing that God has on your life. You shall speak a word from your belly and it shall come to pass. Every thing you touch shall be blessed. Every seed you have planted shall reap a harvest before this year is up in the name of Jesus. I claim victory over the enemy right now in the mighty name of Jesus. I declare and decree that no weapon that has been formed against my family and me shall prosper in the name of Jesus. Lord I thank you again for speaking a word to me this morning that my joy was restored and my peace was reactivated in the name of Jesus. I give you the praise and the glory in Jesus name. Glory to your name Father. You are worthy of the praise and the glory in Jesus name I pray. Amen.

"Praise the Lord, O my soul; all my inmost being, praise his holy name. Praise the Lord, O my soul, and forget not all his benefits, who forgives all your sins and heal all your diseases who redeems your life from the pit and crowns you with love and compassion, who satisfies your desires with good things so that your youth is renewed like the eagles." (Psalm 103:1-5) NIV

My God,

Thank you for all the benefits that come from obeying and doing your will. Thank you for my health, and my strength. Thank you Lord for my family and my friends. Thank you Lord for deliverance in all of our life. Thank you for removing me from the pit of hell. Thank you for ordering my steps and directing my pathway. Thank you for hiding me behind the cross daily. Thank you Lord, for you saving grace. Thank you for touching my eyes that I may see what you would have me to see. Thank you for touching my ears that I only hear what you say to me and not what the world is saying. Thank you for lifting me up when I am down. Thank you for the joy of the Lord is my strength. Thank you for being my redeemer. Thank you for blessing me with a job, that you have placed me on and no man can remove me from. Thank you Lord, that you have established me in all my ways. Thank you for preparing a table before my enemies. Thank you for surrounding me with real godly people, people who want to see me go high and high in you. Thank you for blessing my family with more than enough. Thank you Lord, that we are debt free and walking in prosperity. Thank you for giving me my zeal back for the ministry. Thank you for covering me and my family with your precious blood each day of our life. Thank you for opening doors that man said would not open. Thank you for your darling son Jesus, who died so that I may have the right to the tree of life, and took all my sins and pain with him. Lord, if I had ten thousand tongues it still would not be enough to tell you thank you for all that you do and all that you are about to do in my life. Lord, I love you and appreciate you so much more and more each day. Lord, I will forever give you the praise and the glory in Jesus name I pray. Amen.

"Believe me when I say that I am in the Father and the Father is in me; or at least believe on the evidence of the miracles themselves. I tell you the truth, anyone who has faith in me will do what I have been doing. He will do even greater things than these, because I am going to the Father. And I will do whatever you ask in my name, so that the Son may bring glory to the Father. You may ask me for anything in my name, and I will do it." (John 14:11-14) NIV

"Believe me: I am in my Father and my Father is in me. If you can't believe that, believe what you see—these works. The person who trusts me will not only do what I'm doing but even greater things, because I, on my way to the Father, am giving you the same work to do that I've been doing. You can count on it. From now on, whatever you request along the lines of who I am and what I am doing, I'll do it. That's how the Father will be seen for who he is in the Son. I mean it. Whatever you request in this way, I'll do." (John 14:11-14) Message Bible

Heavenly Father,
    I bow and worship and praise before You and I apply the Blood of Jesus Christ over myself, each person that I have prayed for today; from the tops of our heads to the soles of our feet. I apply the Blood of Jesus over each of us, over the airways that surround us, over us and under us, over telephone lines, over our homes, properties, offices, cars, trucks, businesses, finances, marriages, ministries, cell phone frequencies, and I ask You to render powerless and harmless and nullify the power, destroy the power, cancel the power of any evil spirit, demonic spirit, demonic strongman, messenger of Satan and witchcraft prayer that tries to come into our presence, our homes, everything in our homes, our pets, our properties, our cars, our trucks, everything in our cars and trucks, our marriages, our finances, our ministries, our telephone lines, our telephone frequencies… in the Name of Jesus Christ.

Lord Jesus Christ, I ask You to wash and cleanse my mind with Your Precious Blood. Give each of us clarity of thought; give each of us a sound and sober mind, in Jesus Christ Holy Name; according to John 14:14. To God be the Glory. Amen

"Arise, cry out in the night, as the watches of the night begin; pour out your heart like water in the presence of the Lord. Lift up your hands to him for the lives of your children, who faint from hunger at the head of every street." (Lamentations 2:19) NIV Bible

"As each night watch begins, get up and cry out in prayer. Pour your heart out face-to-face with the Master. Lift high your hands. Beg for the lives of your children who are starving to death out on the streets." (Lamentations 2:19) Message Bible

Oh Lord,
    Giver of light, life and hope, you have entrusted your children to our care. We cherish their love and their energy for life. Help us to help them be the men and women of strength, character, and integrity. Share with us the wisdom that will shape their minds. Share with us the love that will guide their hearts. Share with us the courage that will shape their future. Be the light that guides them and us to your glory and goodness. Lord, we come committing our children unto you. In committing our children to you Lord, an issue of the heart, we are essentially saying several things. We recognize that you are the true and living God. We recognize the need for Your wisdom and strength to raise our children. We desire Your Lordship over their lives, and we desire that our children walk in the ways of the Lord. Many children will be entering kindergarten next school year; some may be taking the SAT test or have already taken it. Some maybe preparing to go off to colleges or universities. Whatever it is or wherever they maybe headed we as parents, as intercessors need to cover all the children in prayer. Lord, we pray that you give each of us wisdom to know how to encourage the children's, so that they can begin to overcome any obstacles that may come their way. Lord, provide the wisdom so that the child who is getting ready to take the SAT or getting ready to go off to college or a university can overcome any and all anxieties. Father we, pray and ask that you cover the children with your blood and that you put and edge of protection around them while they are on summer break. Crown their heads with much wisdom and knowledge of your word during the summer that they will be able to stand the test from the enemy. Give them a keen sense of discernment in the

mighty name of Jesus we pray. Thank you for your love for the children, and your protection over them. Thank you for guiding each of to pray for the children today and everyday in Jesus name we pray. Amen

About the Author

Minister Debra Coleman-LeBum was born in San Antonio, Texas. She is an active member of CRM City Fellowship Church in the Woodlands, Texas; under the leadership of Pastor Leroy J. Woodard Jr. At CRM City Fellowship Church she is Academic Director/Advisor for the Koinonia Theological College. She is also the wife of the Senior Deacon of the Woodlands Campus, an Intercessory, and part of Pastor's Personal Care Counselor. She was called into the ministry in September 2001, and was ordained in May 2003. She has a strong passion for women who are hurting, going through in their marriages, and helping them to overcome all obstacles in their life with the Word of God. She loves the Lord with all my heart, and love working for Him, because she knows that "what she does for the Lord will pay off after while.

Minister LeBum also has another ministry that God has given her outside of her church home. She is the Director/Founder of the "Prayer for Today's Journey Ministry". This is a ministry that God birthed in her right after her mother went home to be with the Lord. This ministry send out a prayer and a scripture to family, friends, and sometimes even strangers, it helps to encourage, to strengthen, and to motivate God's people in there walk with Him. Since March of 2003, she has sent out over 1000 emails each weekday, and has received various emails back on how this ministry has help to change someone's life. To God be the Glory for all that he has done in this ministry. Because it was immediately after her mother passing, that God gave her this ministry it has also helped to strengthen her through it all.

In the fall of 2002, God birth a business into the LeBum family, which is called **CHRIST AND ME (CAM).** They specialize in wedding invitations, business cards, programs, and etc.. Minister LeBum went to the Lord in prayer asking God what to name this business because she *wanted it to include her children's name and at that time her only granddaughter name. That is where the initials come in after the name it stands for her only daughter, her only son, and her granddaughter name (**C**hanikka, **A**lfred Jr, and **M**iyah). God gave me this scripture for the business,* **Philippians 4:13 "I can do all things through Christ Jesus who strengthen me."** *It is a scripture that she lives by daily.*

Minister Debra Coleman-LeBum is married to Deacon Alfred LeBum Sr. They have been married for 30 years and have two wonderful children together. All in all she had five children and eleven grandchildren and two great-grand. She is a graduated of Huston-Tillotson College in Austin, Texas with a B.S. in Business Administration.

Minister Debra LeBum is never too busy for the Lord and his work, she will go where he sends her, and do whatever God ask of her to do. Everywhere she goes she likes to tells people how good God is. Because working for the Lord is her number one priority in life.

To contact Minister Debra Coleman LeBum you may do so by visiting her websites.

Websites:

www.prayersfortodaysjourney.ning.com

www.mychurch.org/minlebum

Words from the Author

Prayer is communicating with God. Talking to God about the things that are weighing you down. Prayer unlocks doors for you. Prayer is your answer. When you have tried to handle that situation or that problem in your life and it doesn't come out right. I dare you to kneel in prayer and ask God to come into your heart. If you have not accepted Jesus Christ as your Lord and Savior, and would like to please pray this prayer with me:

Heavenly Father, I come to you admitting that I am a sinner. I ask that you cleanse me from all unrighteousness. I believe that Your Son, Jesus, dies on the cross to take away my sins. I call upon the name of Jesus Christ to be Savior and Lord over my life. I choose to follow you and ask that you fill me with the power of the Holy Spirit. I declare that right now I am a child of God; I am free from sin and full of the righteousness of God. I am saved. Thank you God for allowing me to repent and be saved in Jesus name I pray. Amen.

If you prayed this prayer to receive Jesus Christ as your Savior for the first time, please ask God to lead you to a spirit filled church so that you can continue to be feed the word of God. God Bless you.

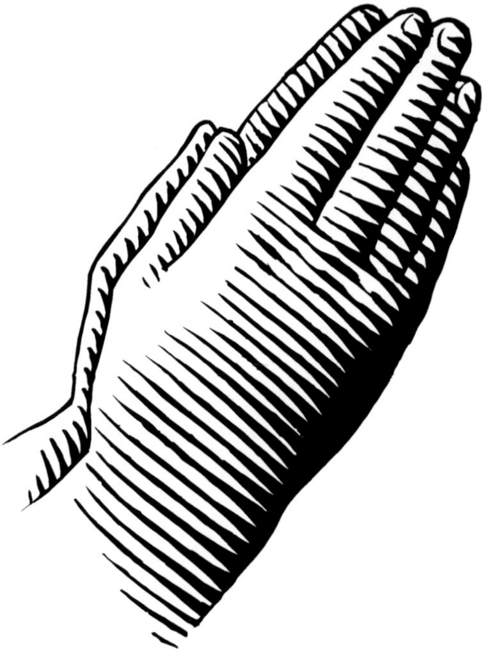